PROBLEMS OF ETHICS

CHANDLER PUBLICATIONS IN PHILOSOPHY
Ian Philip McGreal, Editor

Problems
of
Ethics

Ian Philip McGreal

Sacramento State College

CHANDLER PUBLISHING COMPANY

An Intext Publisher • Scranton, Pennsylvania 18515

CONTENTS

PREFACE

The study of ethics derives its content—and often its direction and inspiration—from the reading of philosophical books and essays by great western thinkers. But far too many students attempt to read Plato, Aristotle, and Kant, as well as other giants in the philosophy of morality, without ever having prepared themselves by acquiring a basic understanding of the problems of ethics, or of the various kinds of proposals that have been made in the attempt to resolve the problems of ethics. Too many students are even unfamiliar with the vocabulary by the use of which philosophers make distinctions that are missed by those limited to ordinary discourse. The remedy appears to be a brief explanatory text which first of all sets forth *the problems of ethics*—the perennial questions concerning good and evil, right and wrong, virtue and vice—that have prompted philosophers to examine, as carefully as possible, the matters to which the language of value and morality calls attention.

An introductory text, preparing the student for the understanding of original works in ethics, would then examine and explain *the most influential and characteristic positions* set forth by the outstanding philosophers of morality. And common sense, which keeps the interests and needs of beginning students in mind, quite naturally demands that the philosophers represented be discussed in *chronological order*, so that some sense of the historical development of ethical thought will result from the student's intellectual passage from Plato through Aristotle, Epicurus, Epictetus, Hume, Kant, Mill, and Moore, to Ayer.

Such an intellectual survey, which has as a side benefit the acquisition of a *working technical vocabulary* to be put to further use in the reading of original essays, provides the student with a dramatic appreciation of the *dialogical character of philosophical thought*. Reason and sentiment, law and man, principle and circumstance, virtue and pleasure—each pair has its moments of emphasis in the thoughts of the philosopher; each member of each pair is in ascendancy at some time, or at a number of times, in the history of philosophical ideas.

My objective has been to write an introductory text of the kind described above. My hope and expectation is that teachers of ethics will move their students from this brief account—designed to provide a clarifying baptism in the fundamentals of ethics and ethical thought—to the great statements which stand as the classics in ethics.

I hope also that this book will be a fit companion for those similar surveys—of problems, philosophers, and positions—which together form the Chandler series of introductory texts, *Problems of Philosophy*. Any student who comes to philosophy by electing either a general introduction or a beginning course in one of the specific fields of philosophy will, we hope, profit from the orientation that these explanatory texts provide.

I. P. M.

PROBLEMS OF ETHICS

I

❧❦❧

THE PROBLEMS
OF ETHICS

Ethics, as one of the fields of philosophy, may be defined as the *philosophy of morality.*

A more extended definitive account calls attention to the features of morality with which philosophy, as ethics, deals: *Ethics* is that branch of philosophy which critically examines, clarifies, and reframes the basic concepts and presuppositions of morality in general.

Specifically, ethics is the attempt to abstract, clarify, and examine the ideas of good and evil, right and wrong, duty and obligation.

The problems of ethics, then, tend to fall into three basic classes: problems about value and basic goods, problems about rightness and wrongness, and problems about moral obligation. But in ethics there are many other problems, derivative from the basic problems, some of them having to do with development of the basic ideas, and others concerning the methods of moral judgment.

For example, philosophers have many questions to ask in the attempt to clarify and appraise the claim that "Murder is always morally wrong."

In considering the claim "Murder is always wrong," the philosopher may ask, "How is the expression 'morally wrong' used in this claim? What does the expression mean? Is the expression, in fact,

1

meaningful? May it not be that the proponent of the claim is merely expressing his own feelings or attitude with regard to murder?

"Or is the person who calls murder 'wrong' only calling attention to the custom, socially established, of looking with disfavor upon, and responding with punitive action to, acts of murder? Are judgments which we tend to describe as 'moral' judgments nothing more than practical decisions which society makes for its own benefit?

"However, it may be that the expression 'morally wrong' has a use which gives moral judgments a meaning and method of verification that can be discovered through experience. It may be that the term 'wrong' involves an implicit reference to some universal law, more fundamental than civil law, and binding upon all men. Is there any such implicit reference in this case? Is there any moral law? Can a legitimate distinction be made between *moral* considerations and *practical,* or expedient, considerations?"

The philosopher continues his questioning of the meaning and justification of the claim that murder is always wrong: "Does the claim that murder is always wrong assert anything about human conduct? Does it not, for example, assert that murder *ought not* to be done? Does it not suggest that a person is always 'morally obligated' to restrain himself from acts of murder?

"And what, in any case, is *murder*? What is meant by the term 'murder'? Can it be that the term 'murder,' as used in the judgment that murder is always wrong, is so used that it would be a contradiction in terms to *deny* that murder is morally wrong? If an act of killing another has some moral justification—whatever that may be—is that act, in virtue of being morally justifiable, *not* an act of murder?

"We really must decide what, if anything, moral justification is. Does justifying an act involve reference to a law, to a judge, to an end or purpose, to a concern—or to what? Or is it possibly meaningless to talk about moral justification? Is the term 'moral justification' really just an instrument in the hands of those who would intimidate others and direct their conduct?

"If it is meaningful to talk about moral justification, does justification involve reference to the good and bad? Is a right act one that is productive of good, and a wrong act one that is productive of the bad? And would moral justification of an act consist in showing that the act did, in fact, produce more good than could have been accomplished in any other way? But how is a person to know what is going to have the best results? And how is a person to decide whether what an act probably will accomplish is really good or really bad? What do the terms 'good' and 'bad' mean? And to what basic or fundamental things or states of being do the terms apply? Is anything worthwhile on its own account?

"Or is talk about the consequences of an act really beside the point? Is a right act simply an act in accordance with fundamental moral principles, whatever may be the outcome of the act? If so, how are moral principles established, and how can they be defended against opposing principles? How is one source of principles to be justified as opposed to some other source, if justification itself involves reference to a principle and source of principles?

"Perhaps the making of moral judgments or of value claims involves reference to persons relative to whom acts are said to be right or wrong, good or bad, obligatory or not. But, if so, to which persons is such reference made? Is the reference in a moral judgment, if there is one, a reference to *the individual making the judgment*? In saying that an act is wrong, is a person suggesting that the act is in some way against his principles, or affects his welfare, or runs counter to the judgment of someone he selects as authoritative?

"Or is the reference in a moral judgment a reference to the moral agent, *the individual whose action is in question*? Is the claim that it is wrong for someone to do a certain kind of act, say murder, a claim that the act so described would be against the principles, inclinations, or judgment of the person being judged?

"Or is the reference neither to the judge nor to the person contemplating the action judged, but to *the persons who would be affected* by the action?

"Or is the reference, implicit in a moral judgment, a reference to *the persons who comprise the society* of which the moral agent is a part?

"Or is the reference, if there is one, a reference to the values or judgments of all mankind? Is a right action one that would be approved by any man, were he to judge without passion or prejudice?

"Or, finally, is the reference to God, as the source of all moral commandments? But, if so, is an act right because God commands it, or does He command it, if He does, because it is right?"

These philosophical questions, prompted by critical reflection on a single moral claim, by no means exhaust the matters to which the philosopher's attention is called by the moral judgments that men make of other men or of what they do. The philosopher of morality, the critic of the ethical ideas and convictions that lie behind the various moral judgments that men make, is interested in exploring the entire area of moral judgment. Some philosophers confine their inquiries to linguistical matters; such philosophers attempt to understand how such terms as "right" and "wrong," "good" and "bad," "duty" and "moral" are used, and what their meanings are. Other philosophers attempt to discover or to decide upon basic principles of action, standards of value and duty. Still other philosophers abandon the attempt to discover fundamental moral principles and seek only to enunciate and promulgate a metaphysical faith in some power or divinity that makes morality possible.

The philosopher of morality generally attempts to discover to what degree considerations described as "moral" are limited to matters of human experience, for he is reluctant to speculate about "worlds" beyond the world of verifiable, factual claims, especially since moral claims are presumed to be central to human action. Many contemporary philosophers in ethics, consequently, tend to confine their philosophical investigations to the study of the language of morality. The conviction of such philosophers is that once one understands how the language of morality is used, there are no further questions—or, at least, no questions worth the further attention of the philosopher. Moral claims are easily appraised, so it is contended, once they are understood—which is to say, once the "logic" of moral discourse has been made apparent through discerning the circumstances under which the language of morality is used, as well as the manner in which that language is used.

Traditionally, however, philosophers have gone beyond questions about the language of morality. They have made the effort not only to understand the basic concepts expressed by the language of morality, but also to discover the foundations of morality—the universal values and moral laws which presumably make firm moral judgments possible. Some philosophers have relied on a kind of intellectual insight, or intuition, in the effort to uncover fundamental, absolute moral principles, while others have frankly speculated by positing a supernatural moral authority and presuming a "world" of freedom and immortality beyond the world of everyday experience.

Between the extremes—between the purely linguistical philosopher and the exclusively metaphysical philosopher—we find the majority of philosophers who, although generally disdaining the speculative dangers of metaphysics, refuse to confine themselves to the study of the uses and meanings of terms used in moral discourse. Such philosophers contend, at least by implication, that significant claims, both meaningful and important, can be made about morality and moral matters, even when such claims are not simply the products of linguistical analysis. Generalizations about the good life, as well as about goodness, the abstract property, are possible.

The concern of the majority of philosophers, then, is not with specific moral judgments of particular men or acts; nor is the concern exclusively with either linguistical matters or metaphysical problems. Most philosophers are interested in the conditions of morality—the factors that make moral judgments possible and with reference to which moral claims can be appraised. For such philosophers, responsible philosophy consists in the creative use of the discoveries made possible through linguistical philosophy, as informed by close attention to the variety of human conditions and concerns.

The philosopher of morality, working within that area of philosophy called "ethics," directs his attention to certain basic problems related to morality. Like other men, the philosopher is acquainted with claims and questions ordinarily described as "moral." The question, "What ought I to do now?" is often used in such a way that the question would customarily be described as a "moral" question—a question for "morality" to answer. The philosopher is interested in knowing what, if anything, distinguishes questions said to be "moral" from questions of other kinds—practical questions, logical questions, scientific questions. And the philosopher also wants to know what, if anything, would count as evidence for the truth of an answer to a moral question.

How, for example, is one to determine whether claims of the following kind—claims that would ordinarily be described as "moral" claims or judgments—are true? "You ought to help the poor old lady by carrying her bundles." "It was wrong of you to hit him in the head." "You have a moral obligation to repay that debt." "You were a bad boy when you lied to your mother." "Every man ought to obey the Ten Commandments, whether or not it is to his advantage to do so." The philosopher is not interested in finding out whether, in a particular case, a moral judgment is true; but he is concerned to discover whether such judgements *can* be true and, if so, *how* they can be true.

Thus, in setting forth the basic problems of ethics, the philosopher asks: "Does the language of morality make sense, and, if so, how? What is a right act? A wrong act? Is there any way of deciding whether something is good on its own account? What is goodness? What is evil?" And he asks, "What can I claim, with philoosophical justification—that is, with experience, language, and logic on my side—about these matters?"

Let us, then, divide the problems of ethics into three basic classes (not necessarily exhaustive, although permitting, in creative hands, the inclusion of almost any ethical problem):

1. *Problems about Duty*: What is moral obligation? When is an act a duty? What makes an act morally right or morally wrong? What is the source and justification of moral principles? Is there a fundamental, universal moral law?

2. *Problems about Value*: What is the distinction between goodness and badness? How is the difference between something good and something evil determined? Is value a matter of opinion, interest, attitude, custom or law? If goodness is a characteristic of some things, acts, or persons, is it analyzable?

3. *Problems about the Good*: Is there anything good for its own sake—good on its own account—quite apart from any value it might have as a means to something else? If something is worthwhile on its own account, does the amount of its value depend on quantity only, or must qualitative differences also be taken into account?

We shall now consider, in some detail, what each of these basic problem areas within ethics involves. It is important to realize not only the range and variety of problems within ethics, but also the degree to which attempts to answer questions within one class involve exploring matters to which attention is called by questions within another class. Problems about duty, for example, usually lead to the consideration of problems about value and the good.

1. THE PROBLEM OF DUTY

The use of such terms as "duty" and "moral obligation" is at first perplexing to philosophers accustomed to talking about the world in terms of physical objects and sensations. There is something familiar, concrete, and, on the face of it, systematically soluble about a problem having to do with the meaning and verifiability of such a claim as "This is a fire." Although philosophers have argued for centuries about proposed answers to the question as to how knowledge of the physical world is possible, few of them have supposed that there is any inherent difficulty in working out an answer.

But the problems of ethics, and particularly problems about duties or moral obligations, take the philosopher out of the comfortable world of sense objects, sensations, predictive claims, and confirmation by perceptual testing. To determine some matter of fact in the perceptual world—as, for example, that the grass is green—one has only to look and see. There may be questions as to what grass is, what looking is, what seeing is, and how conflicts of opinion with regard to the facts are to be settled—but such questions do not appear to be peculiar or puzzling. However, questions as to what duty is, what moral obligation is, what rightness and wrongness are, and how conflicts of opinion with regard to moral matters are to be settled—such questions seem to many philosophers to be especially difficult, peculiar, or puzzling. There is so little understanding or agreement as to what the moral sphere is—and even as to whether there is any such sphere—that some philosophers are inclined to regard questions about duties and obligations as pseudo questions: problems that are insoluble because they are not meaningful to begin with.

Are moral claims verifiable?

One can understand why some philosophers stay clear of ethics altogether. Moral claims cannot be verified by simply using one's eyes, ears, and other sense organs. One begins to wonder whether the language of morality is not just an instrument of intimidation by the use of which some people attempt to control others. The basic problem for the philosopher who inquires about duty and moral obligation, then is to determine whether, in using the terms "duty" and "moral obligation," we are making sense, and, if so, in what way.

It is often supposed by naive thinkers that moral claims about duties and obligations are "merely matters of opinion," the suggestion being that there is no sense in arguing about such matters, for there is no such thing as the correct answer. A moral claim about duty, so such naive commentators charge, is nothing more than the expression of group custom or belief.

But even if this skeptical allegation were true, the problem of determining the *meaning* of moral claims would not be resolved. For even an opinion or custom which has no sanction other than the tendency of a group to hold or practice it is presumably distinguish-

able from opinions or practices that would not be described as
having to do with "duty." Some *customs* are held to be
"obligatory"; the *opinion* is that they are so. But what is the difference between an "obligatory" custom and one which is not, between
a way of acting which is said to be one's "duty" and another way,
perhaps customary, which is merely pleasant or conventional but in
no way "obligatory"?

The tendency to reject as "subjective" any remark which is not
verifiable through sense experience is the product of a primitive
philosophy of science. Surely the belief that if one cannot see something, nothing is there, has long since been shown to be fallacious.
The dogmatic position that if something is the case, it must be "seen
with my own eyes," "seen to be believed," may satisfy those who
live in a simple world of sensation and response, but scientific discourse, like moral discourse, calls attention to more complex matters—matters differing not only in quantity, but also in kind from
the gross objects of everyday sense experience. The electron is discernible (in a sense) because of an intellectual construction that
liberates man from the limited perspective afforded by the use of his
unaided sense organs and the language adapted to the gross methods
of observation. Analogously, it may be argued, duties are discernible
because of intellectual constructions that liberate man from the limited perspective afforded by the exclusive use of his senses, whether
aided or unaided. And the question for the philosopher is the question as to whether this is so: Are duties in some way determinable?
Does discourse about duties in some way make sense? Are claims
with regard to moral obligations in some way verifiable? Granted
that one does not discover the existence and content of duties by
seeing them or smelling them out; granted, also, that relativity physics does not carry us to the realm of rights and obligations—still, the
question remains as to whether duties are not in some way apparent
and in some way confirmable.

Most philosophers have regarded moral discourse as involving the
declaration of claims which are not only meaningful, but also confirmable as true or false, depending upon the circumstances. Nevertheless, a few philosophers—including some of the most influential
contemporary philosophers—have insisted that if moral discourse is
meaningful, it is so only in the sense that it has an emotive or
expressive function. A so-called "moral claim" is a linguistic expression which indicates the speaker's approval of a certain course of
action and urges that course of action upon others. Such discourse is

not verifiable, some hold, because it makes no claims, involves no predictions, and makes reference to no perceptual experience. A statement of the sort, "To do such-and-such is your duty," is more a sign of approval than it is a confirmable description of a publicly observable feature of the act so endorsed.

One of the problems of ethics, then, insofar as ethics is concerned with duty and moral obligation, is the problem of determining whether moral claims about duties are meaningful and, if so, whether they are *empirically* meaningful or only *emotively* meaningful.

Are moral terms definable?

Even if it is conceded that terms such as "duty," "right," and "obligatory" have empirical meanings and descriptive functions, the question remains as to whether the meanings of such terms are *analyzable*. If the term "duty," as used in moral discourse, has utility in describing something so that it makes sense to ask with regard to a moral judgment whether it is true or false, is the term *definable*? Some philosophers have contended that such terms are not definable and that their meanings are not analyzable because the matters designated by such terms are unique and simple. That is, duty is not analyzable because it is not complex; it is not comparable to anything else because it is unique. Other philosophers have held the opposing position, and differences among philosophers who contend that terms of moral obligation are definable consist in differences in the definitions such philosophers propose.

What is the ground of duty?

A third kind of problem about duty is concerned with the question as to the *origin* or *ground* of moral obligation. An act said to be morally obligatory may also be described as morally "imperative" or "necessary." A paradox emerges at this point because, although morally obligatory acts "must" be done since they are "necessary," and necessity is "categorical" or unqualified, at the same time, as we all know, such acts are sometimes *not* performed. Duties are forgotten or ignored; in the struggle between passion and duty, it is not always the latter that prevails. In short, duties need not be done; in some sense they are *not* necessary. The problem, then, is determining *whether* (despite what people say) certain acts are in some way *necessary*. If acts are sometimes morally necessary, *in what way* are they necessary? And if they are in some specified way necessary, what is the *source* of that necessity? Do certain kinds of acts themselves compel (surely in *some* qualified way) performance, or does the necessity of an act's performance lie in the undeniable authority of some moral code or advocate? If it is some authority that requires dutiful action, in what way does that authority create moral necessity? (After all, it would seem that any voice, however eminent, can be disregarded. Is there some sense in which the voice of some authority, say God, *ought not* to be disregarded, not only because such a voice requires what is morally necessary, but also because, in some as yet unspecified way, such a voice creates moral necessity itself?)

It may be that moral necessity is somehow a function of human appetites or interests. Some credibility is given this claim by the consideration that we do sometimes speak hypothetically about the necessity of an act of a certain kind: "*If* you *want* such-and-such, then you *must* do the following." But moral necessity, many philosophers claim—and ordinary discourse provides evidence to support the claim—is not hypothetical, but *categorical*: "You *must* do this act, *whether or not you want to;* there are no 'ifs,' 'ands,' or 'buts' about it!" Nevertheless, it may be that the final support for a moral claim, the force that justifies the assertion of necessity, is the complex of basic human concerns. It may be that a moral claim appeals not to the concerns of the passing moment, concerns provoked in ignorance and without reflection upon consequences, but rather to human interests (whether of an individual or a community) which would be served by informed, calculated action. Perhaps an action is morally imperative if, despite a person's present inclinations, he would undertake the act if only he were aware of the degree to which the consequences of the act would appeal to his basic concerns.

Or, continuing to probe the alternatives in considering the origin or ground of moral necessity, we may find that moral necessity is grounded not in some moral authority, not in the act itself, not in the interests of some agent or community, but in the "principle of the thing," the *form* of the action demanded. Some philosophers (ethical formalists) claim that a principle such as "Tell the truth" is categorically imperative. An act of truth-telling, when the occasion arises for either telling the truth or lying, is said to be morally necessary, whatever one's interests, and whether or not some authority (parents, the state, God) insists upon the act. The necessity of truth-telling is "according to the law, the moral law," and somehow the principle, the moral law itself, generates a demand that cannot be denied. The problem here is to determine whether moral principles and laws are self-justifying sources of moral necessity, and, if so, in what manner.

How is moral knowledge possible?

Another basic problem having to do with duty is the problem of specifying the procedure by which one can acquire knowledge of what ought to be done. Some philosophers argue that a careful subjective "weighing" of a contemplated act is sufficient to yield the conviction that the act is either morally right or morally wrong. In ordinary parlance, the faculty which distinguishes the right from the wrong is called the "conscience." There is a great deal of difficulty, however, in discovering precisely what is meant by the term "conscience," whether there is such a faculty, and, if so, how that faculty works.

Some philosophers say that the faculty of moral discernment—the conscience—works "intuitively." In some "direct" way the seeker after moral truth discovers the rightness or wrongness of acts contemplated. Such a discovery does not involve generalizing upon limited experience or working out the logical implications of empirical results; it is an "immediate" discovery. The act is considered, and then it is "seen" to be morally necessary or, on the other hand, morally wrong. Thus, the moral philosopher is forced (if he is to be exhaustive) to consider what the term "intuition" means, whether there is any such mode of knowledge with regard to moral matters, and, if so, how it operates.

There are many philosophers, of course, who regard moral claims as empirically verifiable. To consider whether an act is morally right or wrong, such philosophers claim, one has only to consider what consequences, or probable consequences, the act will yield if undertaken. Certain kinds of consequences are regarded as constitutive of right action. But the difficulty here is in finding out what sorts of consequences determine right action. Is it *happiness* that makes an act morally right, the required act being the one that yields (or, perhaps, *probably* would yield) the greatest amount of happiness? Or is a right action one that furthers, more than any other, the *realization* or *perfection* of the self or the community? Whatever value is endorsed as being the one that right action fosters, the problem remains as to whether that particular good (happiness, perfection, or whatever) is, as a matter of fact, the final ground of right action, the good by reference to which a moral claim is justified.

The differences in views as to how right actions are to be determined and as to what constitutes the ground of morally obligatory conduct may be summarized by the use of the terms "formalistic" and "utilitarian." A *formalistic* ethics is one in which the final appeal, in defending a claim about duty, is to a *principle* or law—or, possibly, to a "final" authority which is the presumed source of principle or law. A *utilitarian* ethics, on the other hand, appeals not to "the principle of the thing" but to the *consequences* (or probable consequences) of acts. The utilitarian sets forth some feature (said to be worthwhile on its own account), such as happiness or self-realization, as providing the "ground" or ultimate basis for the defense of moral claims. One of the central problems of ethics, then, is the problem of deciding whether the formalist or the utilitarian, or neither, is right in what he says about morally obligatory acts.

2. THE PROBLEM OF VALUE

There is, in ethics, a general problem of value—the problem of deciding what *goodness* and *badness* are. The problem is not that of deciding *what* is good, but, rather, the problem of deciding what *good* is. That is, the problem is not that of deciding what is worthwhile in this life—whether it be happiness, wealth, power, or something else. The general problem of the nature of value, and of goodness in particular, is that of deciding whether there are value characteristics that are the properties of persons, acts, things, or even of ideas—and, if so, how they are to be understood.

Is goodness a property?

The fundamental question concerning value is whether goodness (whatever is meant, if anything, by the adjective "good") is a property or characteristic at all. It may be that the term "good" has no designative function; perhaps the word does not refer to some characteristic belonging to things, acts, persons, or ideas, and does nothing more than express a positive attitude on the speaker's part toward what he indicates as "good."

But even if there is a property, goodness, which is *positive value*, it may be that the property is unique and unanalyzable and that, consequently, the term "good" cannot be defined. Of course, the burden of proof is a particularly difficult one for the proponent of the claim that goodness is unanalyzable, for his point is a negative one. His claim is that, whatever "good" means, the characteristic designated by the term is *not* subject to analysis or clarifying description.

On the other hand, anyone who claims that goodness is analyzable is committed to defining the term "good" so as correctly to bring out the meaning of the term whatever the context.

Is goodness objective or subjective?

If goodness is analyzable (if the term "good" is definable), it is so either by reference to matters *entirely independent of persons* (although it is impossible to comprehend how *any* property, whether or not a value property, can be understood without any reference whatsoever to persons—sentient subjects— as stimulated, affected, or moved by things) or by reference to things *as related to persons.* Things said to be "good" may be related to persons in that the things, when attended to, provoke an interest of some sort, or "good" things may be related to persons simply in virtue of someone's having taken an interest in them.

The philosophical view that value is inherent in objects and is independent of persons may be described as the view that value is "absolutely objective." A view which in some way relates the object, as provoking interest, to someone who consequently finds it valuable, may be said to hold that value is "relationally objective," while the view that objects are in no way involved in a value situation except as objects of interest may be described as involving a "subjective" theory of value.

Thus, there are four alternatives in value theory: either (1) there is no such property as goodness, or (2) goodness is absolutely objective, or (3) goodness is relationally objective, or (4) goodness is entirely subjective.

Even when the decision is made that value terms are definable, the task of analysis and clarification remains. An explanation of value, preferably by definition of the term "good" as used in various contexts, must be constructed which distinguishes positive value from negative value, and value itself from properties other than value.

Is value "unique"?

Part of the argument against the claim that value is analyzable is based on the premise that a property different in kind from empirical, "factual" properties cannot be understood by reference to "factual" matters. Hence, it is argued, value properties, which are presumably quite different from empirical properties such as yellowness and malleability, cannot be analyzed by reference to the senses or in any other way so as not to leave an unexplained and distinctive "value" aspect. Goodness without that unique and unanalyzable value element which makes goodness a value property would not be a kind of value—so some philosophers have claimed. Hence, it is argued, any view which is not circular in the sense of retaining value as an essential element of goodness is fallacious.

But it is characteristic of explanatory definitions that the *definiens* (the defining description) does *not* incorporate the term to be defined or any single term synonymous with the term to be defined. Far from being a weakness, it is usually regarded as a virtue of an analytic report that an analytic definition not include the term to be defined in its account of the parts or aspects uncovered through analysis. The claim that goodness cannot be explained without reference to goodness—that the definition of the term "good" must itself incorporate the term "good" (or a synonym for it)—must be examined critically. Only if value is not subject to analysis which leaves no remainder that is itself the property under investigation, is it the case that it would be a "fallacy" to define value terms in a noncircular fashion.

Intrinsic and instrumental goods

Whether or not the basic term "good" can be defined, certain distinctions are possible which are useful in the discussion of the bearing of value considerations on moral problems. Something may be said to be "good on its own account" or "intrinsically good." The distinction suggested by the expression is that between something that is worthwhile because it is the *means* to something itself worthwhile (the means being describable as an "instrumental good"), and something worthwhile as an *end*, worth having for its own sake. Money, for example, is often instrumentally good, but it is never intrinsically good (not even to the miser, who enjoys it not for its own sake—whatever that might mean—but as a spectacle and a sign of his power). Hedonists claim that pleasure (or happiness) is the only intrinsic good, while anything other than pleasure is good—if it is good—only instrumentally, as a means to pleasure.

The appraisal and endorsement of claims regarding *what*, if anything, is worthwhile on its own account falls within the problem area we have called "The Problem of the Good," but we are here reminded, by the necessity to distinguish between intrinsic and instrumental goods, that the fashioning of terms by which distinctions can be made in the discussion of value is part of what we mean by "The Problem of Value."

3. THE PROBLEM OF THE GOOD

The question as to whether anything is worthwhile on its own account has received a variety of answers. The critical reader of philosophy realizes that philosophers, like other men, are eager to foster their own views of life and its obligations, and hence tend to endorse, as intrinsically good, whatever seems to them to be the final goal of man's striving. Some philosophers mistake instrumental goods for intrinsic ones. Others are so vague or confused in what they say about intrinsic goods that it is impossible to know what they are writing about. Many advance strong opinions, but fail to support them with strong evidence or persuasive reasons.

The problem of the good, like the other problems of ethics, is not to be settled by simple recourse to the great philosophers. Each man must think for himself and must survey various ethical theories as offering views that can be helpful only if soberly appraised by those who temper respect with skepticism. No area within ethics is more likely to challenge the critical thinker than that problem area we have entitled "The Problem of the Good."

Some philosophers have claimed that *virtue* is good on its own account—intrinsically good. Moral virtue or excellence may be instrumentally good—it may bring about desirable states of affairs. But even when virtue, through no fault of its own, goes awry, in that undesirable consequences sometimes result from virtuous acts, some philosophers claim that virtue itself—excellence of moral character—is good on its own account. Other philosophers deny that virtue is ever worthwhile on its own account. It may be inappropriate to blame a *person* whose morally exemplary action has had distressing consequences, but that in no way justifies the claim that moral virtue is itself intrinsically good. If some trait of character is generally productive of beneficial results, if for the most part honesty (for example) leads to human satisfaction and tends to minimize human suffering, then honesty is for the most part good—but only *instrumentally* good.

What is good on its own account, it is often claimed by hedonists and utilitarians, is *happiness*—satisfaction, joy, the feelings of peace, delight, and contentment. And since it is ridiculous to ask what happiness or joy is good *for*, in that the value of happiness is not dependent on the *consequences* of being happy but on the *state* of being happy, happiness can meaningfully and truly be said to be intrinsically good—good on its own account.

But not all philosophers regard happiness as the sole intrinsic good, or even as an intrinsic good at all. Some claim that although it makes sense to talk about aiming at an objective and finding satisfaction in reaching it, the satisfaction is then simply a *sign* of the value of the action; the satisfaction, the pleasure taken in having reached one's objective, is not itself intrinsically good.

Other philosophers, while not denying that pleasure is sometimes worthwhile on its own account, both as a sign of the value of actions and as a reward or consequence of the virtuous or proper exercise of the mind or body, insist that pleasure can be distracting or even bad, leading a person into actions which, however pleasant, cannot be regarded as in any way worthwhile. Since whenever pleasure is morally or instrumentally bad it would be paradoxical to ascribe to pleasure an intrinsic worth, pleasure must have an intrinsic worth only as accompanying worthwhile actions.

Perfection or self-realization is the only intrinsic good, according to another group of philosophers. Sometimes it is the perfection of the "nature" of the individual which is stressed. Sometimes it is the fulfillment of the "destiny" of a social group that is held to be the final or ultimate and intrinsic value. Such a view presupposes the existence of static, predetermined "essences" or "natures," and it assumes that the realization of a given nature is necessarily worthwhile on its own account.

Truth is sometimes regarded as an intrinsic good, although most philosphers would argue that when true belief has value, its value is instrumental. Knowledge and beauty have also been proposed as intrinsic goods, and to such proposals philosophical critics have responded by pointing out that knowledge not used is without value, while a beauty not seen has only a potential aesthetic (hence, instrumental) value.

The philosopher in ethics, the philosopher of morality, may address himself to any or all of the basic problems of ethics. He may attempt to clarify his ideas about duty, moral rightness, and moral obligation; and he may attempt to uncover or prescribe a fundamental moral law by reference to which acts can be appraised. He may seek to understand the world of value—what it is that distinguishes the world as encountered through sense experience from the world as appraised and judged. And he may make the effort to discover, among the multiplicity of goods, those which are ends in themselves, worthwhile on their own account.

These various matters are closely related, and although a philosopher may emphasize one central problem, his presentation usually involves opinions with regard to problems in other areas of ethics.

The student of ethics often begins his effort to resolve the problems of ethics by undertaking a critical survey of philosophical ideas in contention. The great philosophers have offered accounts designed to answer the philosophical questions that have been asked about morality and the language of morality, and it is to the writings of these philosophers that the student turns who would begin the challenging but illuminating task of building clear and useful ideas about the good and bad, the right and wrong, and the range of values to be found in life.

II

PLATO: VIRTUE AS KNOWLEDGE AND HARMONY

For Plato (427–347 B.C.), virtue is knowledge. To know the best is to do the best. Through the study of man, says Plato, one learns that in man there are three fundamental aspects—the rational, the spirited, and the appetitive—which work together effectively only when harmonized. To achieve the harmony of the three aspects of man's nature, music and gymnastics are helpful, for they discipline both the spirit and the body. But the just man most of all seeks the virtues of the soul: wisdom, which is the virtue (or excellence) of the rational element; freedom, the virtue of the spirited element; and temperance, the virtue of the appetitive aspect of man's nature.

The philosopher is one who, as a lover of wisdom, tends to lead the good life (so Plato wrote). He is by profession devoted to justice, and if anyone can teach virtue, it is the philosopher. Nothing can harm him, or any good man, for the just man knows that the goods of the spirit are more important than those of the body. The philosopher is not afraid of death or of dying, for what is important is not subject to change or dissolution. Hence, the true philosopher lives according to the "idea" of the good—that is, by reference to the universal good that forms every particular and individual good. The

19

accidents of time neither depress nor corrupt the philosopher (or any wise and virtuous man), for everything is measured against the unchanging and eternal form of the good. In his social and political life the virtuous man is careful not to injure or corrupt others, for to do so would be to injure the community of which he is a part, and hence to do violence to the idea of justice as harmony.

These views, mediated by the character Socrates in the Platonic dialogues, are central to Plato's ethical thinking. Despite occasional departures from these convictions, departures undertaken in the dialogues for the sake of intellectual testing, Plato fairly consistently held to an ethics based on the central principle that virtue is knowledge. The knowledge which Plato respected, however, was not the practical skill of the technician, but the wisdom of one who, having discovered the forms or ideas of justice and the good, is so drawn to them and to whatever embodies them that he cannot knowingly act in ways opposed to the ideas.

Can virtue be taught?

A characteristic expression of Plato's central proposition is found in his *Protagoras*. Socrates, during the course of a dialogue with Protagoras, a Sophist, refers to the claim made by Protagoras that virtue can be taught. (Protagoras describes himself as a teacher of the art of politics, and he declares that his profession is to make men good citizens by teaching them virtue.) Socrates addresses himself to Protagoras:

You were saying that virtue can be taught. . . . You were speaking of Zeus sending justice and reverence to men; and several times while you were speaking, justice, and temperance, and holiness, and all these qualities, were described by you as if together they made up virtue. Now I want you to tell me truly whether virtue is one whole, of which justice and temperance and holiness are parts; or whether all these are only the names of one and the same thing: that is the doubt that still lingers in my mind.

Protagoras answers by maintaining that "the qualities of which you are speaking are the parts of virtue which is one."

Socrates then asks Protagoras to explain in what sense the various virtues are "parts" of virtue, and Protagoras replies that wisdom, temperance, courage, justice and holiness are parts of virtue in the sense in which the mouth, nose, eyes, and ears are parts of the face. By adroit questioning Socrates forces from Protagoras the admission that folly has two opposites: wisdom and temperance (in that a foolish man is neither wise nor temperate). But nothing has more than one opposite. Therefore, wisdom (which is a kind of knowledge) and temperance must be the same. This conclusion seems to count against the claim that the various virtues are distinguishable parts of a complex whole.

Protagoras then makes the following proposal: ". . . all these qualities are parts of virtue, and . . . four out of the five are to some extent similar . . . [but] the fifth of them, which is courage, is very different from the other four, as I prove in this way: You may observe that many men are utterly unrighteous, unholy, intemperate, ignorant, who are nevertheless remarkable for their courage."

Socrates argues that those who are confident without knowledge "are really not courageous, but mad; and in that case the wisest are also the most confident, and being the most confident are also the bravest, and upon that view again wisdom will be courage."

Protagoras replies that Socrates has not shown that courage is wisdom, for Socrates' argument depends on the premise that confidence and courage are the same. Even though knowledge gives rise to confidence and may, in that way, lead to courage, it does not follow that knowledge is courage, for a man may be confident through "madness" or "rage."

Socrates then suggests that "things are good in as far as they are pleasant, if they have no consequences of another sort, and in as far as they are painful they are bad." The two men thereupon agree to reflect on the claim that "pleasure and good are really the same."

This inquiry is begun by Socrates, who points out that most persons are of the opinion "that a man may have knowledge, and yet that the knowledge which is in him may be overmastered by anger, or pleasure, or pain, or love, or perhaps by fear,—just as if knowledge were a slave, and might be dragged about anyhow." He then asks Protagoras whether he agrees with this common opinion or whether, like Socrates, he thinks "that knowledge is a noble and commanding thing, which cannot be overcome, and will not allow a man, if he only knows the difference of good and evil, to do anything which is contrary to knowledge."

Protagoras states that he agrees with Socrates in thinking that "wisdom and knowledge are the highest of human things," but Socrates reminds the Sophist that most persons believe that men often act contrary to knowledge because they are "overcome by pleasure." But to contend that men sometimes do what they know to be evil because they are "overcome by pleasure" is tantamount to saying that they do what they know to be evil because they are overcome by the good—or that they do what they know to be painful because they are overcome by pleasure. Since neither of these latter propositions is plausible, a further search must be made for the cause of error in the choice of pleasures or goods.

Socrates concludes that men err in their choice of pleasures and pains because they are ignorant of the art of measurement. Many persons are unable to make the right choice of pleasures and pains because they are unable to consider "excess and defect and equality" in the relations of pleasures and pains to one another. If a man chooses a course of action which leads to more pain than pleasure, it is because he is ignorant of the degree to which the remoter pain exceeds the more immediate pleasure. To be "overcome by pleasure," then, is to be misled, not by pleasure, but by ignorance.

Honorable and useful acts, Socrates concludes, are those the tendency of which is to make life painless and pleasant. He argues that "if the pleasant is the good, nobody does anything under the idea or conviction that some other thing would be better and is also attainable, when he might do the better. And this inferiority of a man to himself is merely ignorance, as the superiority of a man to himself is wisdom."

Socrates has made clear the reasons he has for maintaining that men err through ignorance. He reaffirms his conclusion by declaring, ". . . no man voluntarily pursues evil, or that which he thinks to be evil. To prefer evil to good is not in human nature; and when a man is compelled to choose one of two evils, no one will choose the greater when he may have the less."

Protagoras is reminded that he has claimed that courage is different from the other virtues in that intemperate and ignorant men are sometimes courageous. Socrates now argues that the confidence of the coward is a "base" confidence, which originates in ignorance. Cowards who rush into danger through ignorance can hardly be said to be courageous. The courageous man, on the other hand, goes into battle because he knows it to be honorable and good; his virtue consists in his knowledge of the good to be won through action.

The conclusion of the *Protagoras* is a characteristic passage of Socratic irony. The dialogue is built around the question as to whether virtue can be taught. Socrates points out that he has been making the effort to deny Protagoras's claim that virtue can be taught, but by insisting that virtue is knowledge Socrates has, in effect, suggested that virtue *can* be taught. Protagoras, on the other hand, initially defended the claim that virtue can be taught, but in arguing that courage is different from the other virtues, in that ignorant men can be courageous, he has, in effect, maintained that virtue *cannot* be taught. The question is recognized as one that needs further investigation, but the dialogue closes with the agreement between Protagoras and Socrates to meet again and discuss the matter further.

What is justice?

In the *Republic*, Plato, once again using Socrates as the philosophical center of a searching dialogue, explores the problem of duty by having various disputants respond to the question "What is justice?" Cephalus suggests that justice consists in speaking the truth and paying one's debts, but Socrates shows, by a clear exception, that Cephalus is mistaken:

Suppose that a friend when in his right mind has deposited arms with me and he asks for them when he is not in his right mind, ought I to give them back to him? No one would say that I ought or that I should be right in doing so, any more than they would say that I ought always to speak the truth to one who is in his condition . . . .

By showing that under certain circumstances it would not be right to restore to its owner something one has been given in trust, Socrates rejects the general account by which Cephalus attempted to explain what duty, justice, or rightness is. The attempt throughout, by all concerned, is not to decide whether a particular kind of act would be right or wrong but to discover a *feature common to dutiful acts* (acts in accordance with justice) by reference to which a *definition* can be framed. When Cephalus concedes that Socrates has found a legitimate objection to the theory that justice consists in the repayment of debts and the telling of the truth, Socrates comments, "But then . . . speaking the truth and paying your debts is not a correct definition of justice."

Polemarchus then enters the discussion by claiming that the view held by Simonides—namely, that justice is "the giving to each man what is proper to him . . . "—provides the correct definition of justice. Polemarchus explains the expression "giving to each man what is proper to him" by redefining justice as follows: ". . . justice is the art which gives good to friends and evil to enemies."

Socrates objects to this proposal by arguing that to give evil to a man is to injure him "in that which is the proper virtue of man . . . "; namely, in respect of justice. Hence, to injure a man is to make him unjust. Thus, justice can hardly consist in giving evil to enemies, for to do so would be to create injustice. Furthermore, there are difficulties arising from the fact that men err in their judgments of others, and often the persons who are our friends are not, in fact, good, while the ones we regard as our enemies may not have the vices we attribute to them.

Thrasymachus then proposes that justice be considered to be "the interest of the stronger." Socrates pretends to misunderstand:

What, Thrasymachus, is the meaning of this? You cannot mean to say that because Polydamus, the pancratiast [boxer and wrestler], is stronger than we are, and finds the eating of beef conducive to his bodily strength, that to eat beef is therefore equally for our good who are weaker than he is, and right and just for us?

After declaring to Socrates that "you take the words in the sense which is most damaging to the argument," Thrasymachus explains that what he means to contend is that since laws are made by governments "with a view to their several interests," justice consists in conformity to whatever laws those who are powerful enough to rule have laid down.

Socrates points out that rulers sometimes make mistakes in framing the laws; what the rulers suppose is to their own interest may actually be harmful to them.

Thrasymachus insists that to be the "stronger" is to be a ruler who does not err in the making of laws. The ruler fashions the laws so that his interests are served. Hence, whatever is just is to the interest of the stronger.

Socrates then argues that the art of government is the art of acting for the good of the subject. Just as the art of medicine is the art of utilizing the power and knowledge of the physician for the good of the patient, so the art of government is the art of utilizing the power of the ruler for the good of those who are ruled. Hence, justice cannot consist in doing what is to the interest of the stronger; if anything, it would consist in doing what is in the interest of the weaker.

The task of defining justice is seen to be a difficult and complex one. A series of searching questions leads to the decision that justice is "virtue and wisdom," while injustice is "vice and ignorance." The argument is that the just man does not seek anything more than just action; he seeks to achieve as much justice as possible, and his only interest in exceeding anyone is in overcoming those who, through ignorance, are deficient in virtue. Just as the musician and the medical man confine themselves to what is best in their fields but seek to excel those who, through ignorance, are constantly going beyond the limits of good performance, so the just man, through knowledge and wisdom, limits himself to the good and opposes himself to the bad.

Socrates then defines the "end" of something as "that which could not be accomplished, or not so well accomplished, by any other thing." It is better to be just than to be unjust, Socrates claims, because justice consists in fulfilling the end of the soul, and such fulfillment or excellence is always a cause of happiness.

But the question remains as to what constitutes the virtue or excellence of the soul. Socrates suggests that an inquiry be made into the nature of justice and injustice as they appear in the state. Since the state is larger than the individual, it is more easily studied and analyzed. If it is possible to discover what the distinctive excellence of the state is, it may then be possible to understand what constitutes the virtue or excellence of the individual.

The bulk of the *Republic* consists of a discussion of the state as a complex organization designed to meet the needs of the individuals of which it is composed. Every state needs workers, who supply and transport the necessities of life; warriors, who defend the state against its enemies; and rulers, or guardians, who apply their knowledge to the task of controlling the various kinds of citizens so as to bring about the good of the whole state. Socrates declares that the greatest good of the state is "the bond of unity"; the greatest evil, on the other hand, is "discord and distraction and plurality where unity ought to reign."

In answer to the question as to whether Socrates' description of the state, or republic, is that of the actual or the ideal, Socrates concedes that it is of the ideal. But it is by reference to the ideal that the end of the state is to be understood, and knowledge of the end is necessary if one is to understand the distinctive virtue of the state. Actual states could be transformed by the ideal if one essential condition were satisfied:

Until philosophers are kings, or the kings and princes of this world have the spirit and power of philosophy, and political greatness and wisdom meet in one, and those commoner natures who pursue either to the exclusion of the other are compelled to stand aside, cities will never have a rest from their evils,—no, nor the human race, as I believe,—and then only will this our State have a possibility of life and behold the light of day.

The ideal republic, then, is the state as ruled by philosophers, for the philosopher is the lover of wisdom: " . . . philosophical minds always love knowledge of a sort which shows them the eternal nature not varying from generation and corruption." As lovers of the eternal natures (the "ideals" or "ideas"), philosophers are "lovers of all true being." In the philosopher-king the "vision of truth" is related to the practical arts of government; harmony and unity result when the ruler is one whose virtue is wisdom.

By the simile of a cave, Socrates explains what it is that makes attaining a vision of "true being" so difficult. Human beings are like prisoners in an underground den. They have never seen the world outside, and everything they know is by reference to the shadows of being which the light from outside the cave casts upon the wall before the prisoners. But the prisoners do not realize that the images before them are nothing but copies of true things; since their vision is confined to the wall, they have no suspicion that there is a world of true being beyond, an "intellectual" world which the sun (the "idea of the good") pervades. The philosopher is like one who, having been freed from the cave, comes into the world of eternal forms and finally realizes that the shadows in the cave (the individual things of the world of sense experience) are merely poor copies of the unchanging "ideas."

The ideal soul

An image of the ideal soul is now possible. The ideal soul will be just, and it will recognize—through the examination of the ideal republic—that justice through the harmony of elements is better for a man than injustice. The soul is pictured as resembling a man, but as being nevertheless, a composite of three elements: first, a many-headed monster (the heads being of both tame and wild animals); second, a lion; and third, a man. Those who argue that injustice is more profitable than justice are asserting, in effect, that the man profits by being left to the mercy of the many-headed monster and the lion. The defender of justice as being the more profitable for man affirms, on the other hand, that the good of the soul consists in giving the man mastery over the beasts within.

If a person who is unjust is undetected and unpunished, Socrates points out, he "only gets worse, whereas he who is detected and punished has the brutal part of his nature silenced and humanized; the gentler element in him is liberated, and his whole soul is perfected and ennobled by the acquirement of justice and temperance and wisdom . . . ."

The just soul is "the servant of the best"; such a soul is one in which "the Divine rules . . . ." Just as the law is the principle by which the state is ordered, so in each soul there is, or ought to be, a ruling principle, a law for the ordering of the elements of the soul so that harmony is achieved and the higher is allowed dominance over the lower.

No man is knowingly or willingly unjust, then, for no man who knew what he was doing would corrupt and destroy himself by allowing the beasts within him to dominate. Nor would he be so foolish as to create anarchy within himself, thereby providing the condition of lawlessness by which the lower elements of the soul grow in power and ultimately destroy the integrity of the person.

Is pleasure the chief good?

Although Plato often maintains that the good and virtuous life is a happy one, he is not willing to concede that pleasure is the chief good of life. In the dialogue *Philebus*, Plato represents Socrates as arguing against the view, defended by Philebus, that "pleasure is the true end of all living beings, . . . that it is the chief good of all, and that the two names 'good' and 'pleasant' are correctly given to one thing and one nature . . . ."

Pleasure that is not felt or remembered is without value. But wisdom devoid of pleasure would also be worthless. Neither pleasure nor wisdom without the other would be good. Hence, Socrates concludes, the good must consist of a "mixture" composed of pleasure, "a fountain of honey," and wisdom, "a sober draught . . . of water unpleasant but healthful . . . ."

Socrates inquires into the cause of the best possible mixture of pleasure and wisdom, and he concludes that the cause is threefold; beauty, symmetry, and truth must order the mixture.

The next problem to resolve is that of deciding whether pleasure or mind is more akin to the threefold cause of the highest and best mixture of the two. Since pleasures are often false and immoderate, and pleasant actions often "ridiculous or disgraceful," while the mind is either the same as, or close to, truth, symmetry, and beauty, the conclusion is that it is mind or wisdom that contributes most to the value of the combination under discussion. The Platonic emphasis on harmony is consistent with the claim that virtue is wisdom. The wise man is one who, by attention to and admiration of the "ideas" of the good, true, and beautiful, is naturally inclined to give priority to whatever is most akin to these ideals. Such a man prefers the ordering of elements, or harmony (symmetry), to the disorder which characterizes the behavior of one who is immoderate, unjust, and foolish. He profits from the triumph of man over the beasts within him. Wisdom brings him happiness and enhances his pleasure, and since everything that is worthwhile comes to him as a result of his obedience to the "ideas" which inform his life, he has no fear of injustice or death; his concern is for the soul, and his devotion is to eternal values.

The moral ideal

Plato's dialogue *Apology* is an account of the defense (apology) made by Socrates during his trial by the Athenians who have charged him with impiety and with having corrupted the young. If Socrates is found guilty, the probable penalty will be death, but Socrates declares to the judges that "a man who is good for anything ought not to calculate the chance of living or dying; he ought only to consider whether in doing anything he is doing right or wrong—acting the part of a good man or of a bad." He argues that every state needs critics who will examine the "pretenders to wisdom," and he cautions them that "if you kill such an one as I am, you will injure yourselves more than you will injure me." Socrates describes himself as a "gadfly," given by God to sting the state and arouse it from its lethargy:

And now, Athenians, I am not going to argue for my own sake, as you may think, but for yours, that you may not sin against the God by condemning me, who am his gift to you. For if you kill me you will not easily find a successor to me, who, if I may use such a ludicrous figure of speech, am a sort of gadfly, given to the State by God; and the state is a great and noble steed who is tardy in his motions owing to his very size, and requires to be stirred into life . . . .

He argues that a critic of conventional ideas, one whose mission it is to seek the truth and to bring about the improvement of the soul, must be willing to lose his life:

And do not be offended at my telling you the truth: for the truth is, that no man who goes to war with you or any other multitude, honestly striving against the many lawless and unrighteous deeds which are done in a state, will save his life; he who will fight for the right, if he would live even for a brief space, must have a private station and not a public one.

Declaring that the difficulty in life "is not to avoid death, but to avoid unrighteousness," Socrates argues that death is either "a state of nothingness" or "a change and migration of the soul from this world to another." If death is the journey to the world below, where men are immortal, then, says Socrates, "I shall . . . be able to continue my search into true and false knowledge; as in this world, so also in the next; and I shall find out who is wise, and who pretends to be wise, and is not." Hence, he concludes, "no evil can happen to a good man, either in life or after death."

Socrates is found guilty and is sentenced to death. His last hours, given over to philosophical discussions with his friends, are represented by the Platonic dialogue *Phaedo*, which reports Socrates as spending most of his time in the effort to prove the immortality of the soul. Presuming himself to have shown that the soul, as the life-bearer, cannot admit death and, hence, must be immortal, Socrates attempts to raise the spirits of his followers in a passage which can serve as a summary of the Platonic position in ethics:

Those . . . who have been pre-eminent for holiness of life are released from this earthly prison, and go to their pure home which is above, and dwell in the purer earth; and of these, such as have duly purified themselves with philosophy live henceforth altogether without the body, in mansions fairer still which may not be described . . . .

Wherefore, . . . seeing all these things, what ought not we to do that we may obtain virtue and wisdom in this life? Fair is the prize, and the hope great!

. . . Wherefore, I say, let a man be of good cheer about his soul, who having cast away the pleasures and ornaments of the body as alien to him and working harm rather than good, has sought after the pleasures of knowledge; and has arrayed the soul, not in some foreign attire, but in her own proper jewels, temperance, and justice, and courage, and nobility, and truth—in these adorned she is ready to go on her journey to the world below, when her hour comes.

III

ARISTOTLE:
THE GOOD AS
RATIONAL ACTIVITY

Aristotle (384-322 B.C.) begins his ethics (as represented in the *Ethica Nicomachea*) with an account of the good as "that at which all things aim," and he declares that if there is some end "which we desire for its own sake (everything else being desired for the sake of this)," then that end is "the good and the chief good."

There is a "verbal" agreement as to what the chief good is, Aristotle points out: ". . . both the general run of men and people of superior refinement say that it is happiness, and identify living well and doing well with being happy . . . ." But there is disagreement as to what happiness is, for some men think that a life of pleasure is a happy one, while others maintain that it is a life of wealth or honor.

Aristotle suggests that there are three basic kinds of lives: the life of enjoyment, the life of politics, and the life of contemplation. A life devoted to nothing but pleasure seems more appropriate to the beasts than to man, and hence it is unlikely that pleasure is man's chief good. Honor, which is the end of the political life, depends on those who grant it; hence, it cannot be the chief good, which must be something that depends on a man himself. Virtue is better than honor, but even a life of virtue would not be satisfactory if the virtuous person were inactive or continually suffering. As for wealth, its value is obviously that of a means; it could hardly be the chief good.

Even at the outset of the *Ethica Nicomachea*, then, it appears that the chief good of which happiness consists is to be found in the life of contemplation, for no other basic mode of life seems to guarantee happiness. But before discussing contemplation, Aristotle undertakes a brief criticism of the Platonic theory (with which he was well acquainted, for Plato had been his teacher) that things which are good in themselves are so by reference to a single "idea" or "form." His conclusion is that the idea of good could hardly be the only thing good in itself, for if it were, the idea would be empty; that is, there would be no goods of which the idea would be the form. But goods such as wisdom, honor, and pleasure are distinct and diverse; hence, there is no single idea of the good.

The chief good must be a "final end," according to Aristotle; that is, it must be something "always desirable in itself and never for the sake of something else." It is true that happiness is the chief good and final end, but to say so "seems a platitude," and therefore, if one is to determine what man's happiness consists in, one must determine what his function is.

The good man

Aristotle decides that the function of *man* is "an activity of soul which follows or implies a rational principle," and hence the function of a *good* man is "activity of soul in accordance with virtue, and if there are more than one virtue, in accordance with the best and most complete."

Most of the balance of Aristotle's *Ethica Nicomachea* is devoted to a study of the virtues of man. Aristotle distinguishes two kinds of virtue—the intellectual and the moral—and he lists philosophic wisdom, understanding, and practical wisdom as intellectual virtues, while liberality and temperance are regarded as moral.

Moral virtue is a result of habit, contends Aristotle, but the intellectual virtues result from teaching. Virtues are neither passions nor faculties but "states of character," and any state of character is a virtue if it is an *excellent* state; that is, "the state of character which makes a man good and which makes him do his work well."

Virtue, moreover, is concerned with *choice*, and the right choice is determined by reason, which controls the appetitive part of the soul (in the exercise of moral virtue) and the rational principle itself (in the exercise of intellectual virtue).

The golden mean

The crux of Aristotle's ethics is reached with the claim that reason determines the right course of action by deciding on the "mean" or "temperate" way between the extremes of excess and deficiency. He points out that "fear and confidence and appetite and anger and pity and in general pleasure and pain may be felt both too much and too little, and in both cases not well; but to feel them at the right times, with reference to the right objects, towards the right people, with the right motive, and in the right way, is what is both intermediate and best, and this is characteristic of virtue."

A definition of virtue is then offered: "Virtue ... is a state of character concerned with choice, lying in a mean, i.e. the mean relative to us, this being determined by a rational principle, and by that principle by which the man of practical wisdom would determine it."

A life of moderation is what Aristotle endorses as morally virtuous. In general, the right, virtuous, and excellent course of action is one in which one does neither too much nor too little. But since men and circumstances vary, it is not always easy to determine precisely where the line should be drawn so that one is neither excessive nor deficient in satisfying the passions through action. The solution is to do what a man rationally determining the mean would do. Apparently Aristotle believed that what he called the "rational element" in the soul could weigh the alternative courses of action and choose the temperate course.

Aristotle points out that a ritualistic obedience to the principle of the mean (or middle) course is not enough if one is to achieve moral excellence. If the passion or action one is considering is already an excess or deficiency, hence bad, no mean is possible. One cannot choose the right degree of cowardice, a middle course between being too cowardly or not cowardly enough, for cowardice is already an excess of fear. And just as there is no mean of passions or actions already excessive or deficient, so there is no excess or deficiency of actions or passions already temperate. (There is no such thing as too much temperance.)

Aristotle's doctrine of the "golden mean" is illustrated by a "table" of extremes and means. Courage is the mean between fear and confidence. Temperance is the mean between self-indulgence and what Aristotle (for want of a name in common use) calls "insensibility." The defect of character which leads to the excessive giving of money is prodigality; that which inhibits adequate giving is meanness. The mean between the two is liberality. The mean as far as honor and dishonor are concerned is called "proper pride"; the excess is "empty vanity," and the deficiency is "undue humility." As far as temperament goes, the excess is irascibility, the deficiency is "inirascibility" (the fault of one who cannot get stirred up about anything), and the mean is a good temper.

Other moral virtues and vices are considered by Aristotle, and in each case the virtue is the mean or middle way between the extremes of excess and deficiency.

Justice

Before passing on to a discussion of the intellectual virtues, Aristotle undertakes a detailed analysis of justice. Justice *in general* is obedience to the laws, and insofar as a man follows the moral laws which prescribe the mean, his condition is one of justice or complete virtue: he is just in relation to his neighbor, virtuous in his own character.

Justice *in particular* is concerned with the "fair and equal." A man who takes more than his share of something in order to satisfy himself does what is unfair, and since his act is unfair, it is unjust. But not every unjust act (in the broad sense of "unjust," as meaning "contrary to law") is unfair.

Particular justice is of two kinds: *distributive* (having to do with the distribution of money, honor, or other goods) and *rectifying* (concerned with the transactions between man and man, when the one has wronged the other and there is the necessity for restoring the balance). Aristotle suggests that justice is achieved through the right proportion. In the case of distributive justice, the proportion is geometrical (the relation between persons, who may not be equally deserving, is proportionate to that between the goods distributed). The proportion involved in rectifying justice, however, is not geometrical but arithmetical (in that the problem for a judge in attempting to restore the balance of goods when one man has wronged another is that of subtracting from the wrongdoer whatever he has gained from the victim and then restoring to the victim what he has lost). Aristotle's examples suggest that he was aware of the difficulty of achieving the proper proportion in cases in which equality cannot be achieved by the simple transfer of goods. The judge, says Aristotle, is called a "mediator" because his function is that of determining the intermediate, or just proportion. One concludes that more is needed than a formula; justice is achieved through the use of reason only after a sensitive appraisal of particular circumstances.

Unjust acts and unjust men

An act may be unjust (wrong), Aristotle points out, and yet the person who commits the act need not be unjust (morally at fault). A man acts unjustly not simply by doing an unjust act but by doing it voluntarily or intentionally. Only voluntary acts are properly blamed or praised. If an act (like that of striking one's father) is accidental or under compulsion, or is done from ignorance, then, according to Aristotle's definition of "voluntary," the act is not voluntary. Such an act would be unjust, but the person who committed the act would not have acted unjustly; he would not be subject to blame, for he would not have acted by choice.

An important distinction is made between acting *from* ignorance and acting *in* ignorance. If passion, rather than ignorance, is what leads a man to act unjustly, then (even if he is ignorant) his act is not excusable.

Since voluntary acts may be done either "by choice" or "not by choice"—that is, either deliberately or not—an account of the relationship between unjust acts and unjust men becomes possible for Aristotle. Whenever a man acts unjustly *by choice*, he is an unjust man, but if, although he acts unjustly, he does not do so deliberately, he is not himself unjust.

When an injurious act turns out to have had consequences other than those one might reasonably have expected, it is not an unjust act but a "misadventure." When an injury, although one might reasonably have expected it to occur, is nevertheless not the result of deliberation, it is a "mistake." A man acts unjustly when he acts "with knowledge but not after deliberation" (as, for example, when he acts angrily), but the man himself is unjust only when his act is deliberate, "from choice."

The intellectual virtues

Aristotle contends that there are two ways of grasping a principle intellectually. The *scientific* way is appropriate to matters which are invariable; the deliberative or *calculative* way is appropriate wherever there is variation. Since, as Aristotle characteristically puts it, the "virtue of a thing is relative to its proper work," there must be intellectual virtues which are understandable as the best or highest states of the two functions of reason.

The scientific or contemplative reason aims at the truth, while the deliberative or calculative reason, at its best, is in accord with right desire.

The intellect, or rational part of man, has an important part to play in the making of moral choices, for if a man is to be just—that is, if he is deliberately to do the right thing—he must grasp the truth through the use of contemplative reason, bring truth into agreement with desire through the deliberative and practical reason, and act accordingly by choice. Aristotle emphasizes the complex character of moral action by declaring that "choice cannot exist either without reason and intellect or without a moral state; for good action and its opposite cannot exist without a combination of intellect and character." The contemplative reason uncovers the *end* of action; it is philosophic in that it grasps what is "universal and necessary." The deliberative intellect, on the other hand, discovers the *means* of action; it is practical in that it lays down courses of action. Intuitive reason and practical wisdom must both be operative if man is to be guided properly in the making of choices.

Knowledge and virtue

Aristotle considers the Socratic view that knowledge is virtue—that is, that no man who knows what is best acts in some way that falls short of the best; to know what is best is sufficient for doing what is best.

The "observed facts," says Aristotle, suggest that Socrates was mistaken. It often appears to be the case that although a man knows what is the right thing to do, he does something else instead. Aristotle then proceeds to show that it is possible for a person who knows what is best to do something else.

Sometimes a man knows what is best in the sense that he has the knowledge, but he may choose the unjust act because, although he has the knowledge, he does not use it. Or a man may have knowledge of a general principle but fail to apply it in a particular case. Or a man who has knowledge may, while under the influence of some passion, such as anger, forget what he knows. Or a general rule of conduct may be set aside because a person's opinion about some particular thing provokes an appetite that leads to action which prevents any consideration of the bearing of the universal principle on what he is doing.

Aristotle's answer to Socrates, then, is that if knowledge is to be influential in moral conduct, it has to be realized and exercised. Knowledge must be active if it is to have any force; it has to be recalled and put to use. Yet men may know and not bring their knowledge to bear on problems; they may not use their knowledge properly; they may allow knowledge of what appeals to them at the moment to take priority over broad moral principles. Sometimes a man knows only in the sense that he can talk and give the right answers to questions; his talk is then empty and has nothing behind it by which he can be influenced in what he does.

To be continent or morally restrained, then, a person must develop habits by which his rational side can prevail over his irrationally directed appetites. The incontinent man is one who is overcome by passion, but he does not suppose that he ought to pursue the excessive and unjustified pleasures that become his end. Incontinence is better than self-indulgence, therefore, for the self-indulgent man not only pursues excessive pleasures (thereby violating the rule of moderation), but also supposes that he is right in doing so. The criminal or wicked man is distinguishable from both the incontinent and the self-indulgent man, for the criminal (or vicious man) is not only overcome by passion in the violation of the rules of action, but also acts with malice and by choice.

Pleasure and morality

Aristotle maintains that "moral virtue and vice are concerned with pains and pleasures . . . ." He offers in defense of his claim the fairly obvious consideration that "it is on account of the pleasure that we do bad things, and on account of the pain that we abstain from noble ones." In any case, since happiness "involves pleasure," it is relevant to a study of ethics, then, to consider whether pleasure is a good—the chief good—and what relation pleasure has to morally significant action.

Three views relating to pleasure are carefully examined by Aristotle: the view that pleasure is never good; the view that although some pleasures are good, most are bad; and the view that even if pleasure is good, the *summum bonum* (highest good) cannot be pleasure.

Aristotle cites the following claims as having been made in defense of these views: pleasure cannot be identified with the good; pleasure is a "process" leading to the restoration of a natural state; the temperate man avoids pleasure; practical wisdom aims at the avoidance of pain, not the acquisition of pleasure; pleasures hinder thought; there is no art of pleasure; both children and brutes pursue pleasure; most pleasures are either base or harmful.

Aristotle argues in rebuttal that the reasons given are not sufficient to show that pleasure is not a good, or even that is is not the chief good. He suggests that the reason why some critics think that pleasure is not good at all is that they consider pleasures (pleasant activities) to be simply good or bad, without realizing that the worth of an activity varies from person to person and according to circumstances. Furthermore, such critics tend to concentrate on some harmful activity, said to be pleasant, and use the isolated example as evidence for the view that pleasure is never good.

Aristotle denies that pleasure is the process of restoration to a natural state. Pleasure arises not from "becoming something, but when we are exercising some faculty . . . ." Pleasures are better describable as "activities and ends," and hence it is more likely that pleasure is a good as an end than that it is merely an incidental accompaniment of a restorative process.

Aristotle also denies that pleasure is an art. An art, he points out, relates to a faculty, and not to pleasure as an activity. The activity of cooking may be pleasant (as may the activity of eating), but it is only the ability to cook that can meaningfully be described as artful.

Some critics argue that pleasure impedes practical wisdom and interferes with thinking and learning. But, Aristotle argues, "the pleasures arising from thinking and learning will make us think and learn all the more."

In response to the claim that the man of practical wisdom aims at the avoidance of pain rather than the acquisition of pleasure, Aristotle suggests that although the man of practical wisdom, who is a man of temperance, avoids harmful pleasures, including excessive bodily pleasures, he does pursue and enjoy the pleasures of temperate activities.

The philosopher calls attention to the fact that most persons agree that pain is bad and is to be avoided. But pleasure is the opposite of pain. Consequently, pleasure is good.

Even if some pleasures are bad, it may be that the chief good is pleasure of some sort. Since happiness consists in unimpeded activity in the fulfillment of one's end, pleasure must be an essential part of happiness, for it is unimpeded activity.

Aristotle's conception of the happy life is one that recognizes the range of factors that may impede the exercise of a man's faculties:

And . . . all men think that the happy life is pleasant and weave pleasure into their ideal of happiness—and reasonably too; for no activity is perfect when it is impeded, and happiness is a perfect thing; this is why the happy man needs the goods of the body and external goods, i.e. those of fortune, viz. in order that he may not be impeded in these ways . . . .

Characteristically, Aristotle argues that the alternative to seeking the excessive pleasures of the self-indulgent man is not the avoidance of pleasures altogether, but the pursuit of a properly temperate exercise of the human faculties. As proper to man and limited by practical wisdom the activities which avoid excess are both useful and pleasant.

Friendship and the good life

Aristotle emphasizes the importance of friendship by devoting two chapters of the *Ethica Nicomachea* to the subject. The good and virtuous life is not possible without friends. Friendship is necessary not only because of what it contributes to the well-being of those immediately involved, but also because of what it adds to the strength and value of the state. So powerful is the effect of friendship that, claims Aristotle, "when men are friends they have no need of justice, while when they are just they need friendship as well . . . ."

Three kinds of friendship are discussed by Aristotle. Things are loved if they are lovable in that they are useful, pleasant, or good. Friendship, then, may be for utility, for the sake of pleasure, or for the sake of the good. In neither of the first two cases is the friendship based upon a love of the other for himself, and hence when the friendship is no longer useful or pleasant, it is dissolved. "Perfect friendship," on the other hand, writes Aristotle, "is the friendship of men who are good, and alike in virtue, for these wish well alike to each other *qua* good, and they are good in themselves."

Aristotle's conception of friendship is broader than that idea associated with the modern use of the term "friendship." By friendship Aristotle means a concern for the other, even though that concern may be comparatively impersonal and unemotional. The relationship between friendship and justice is consequently very close. The virtuous man achieves justice in his relationships with others when what moves him is the virtue of the other.

If a man is to secure what is good *for* himself, then, he must be friends with others not because of the utility or pleasantness of the other, but because of the virtue in the other. What, finally, is good for a virtuous man is whatever is good for his friends. On the level of friendship based on the good, no distinction can be drawn between what is good for the individual as an individual and what is good for him as a friend and citizen. If everyone were to engage only in noble actions and thereby to make the good and noble more important than satisfying the appetite for what is excessive, then, says Aristotle, "everything would be as it should be for the common weal, and every one would secure for himself the goods that are greatest, since virtue is the greatest of goods."

Perfect happiness as contemplation

The conclusion hinted at in the beginning of the *Ethica Nicomachea* is finally made explicit in the persuasive argument which makes up Book X of Aristotle's treatise. Happiness is activity in accordance with virtue, and man's virtue—or distinctive excellence—is the use of the contemplative reason. Happiness, therefore, consists in the exercise of the faculty of contemplation.

Aristotle points out that the practical virtues, exercised in the conduct of political or military affairs, are by their very nature, as instrumental toward ends, unleisurely. Yet happiness depends on leisure, he argues, "for we are busy that we may have leisure, and make war that we may live in peace."

The activity of contemplative reason, on the other hand, is an end in itself; it is a leisurely activity involving the highest faculty of man and having as its objects the best of all that is knowable. Consequently, the life of contemplative reason is the supremely happy life. A life of exclusively practical activity or of pursuits for the sake of amusement would not be a happy life for, if man is to be happy, he must do what is proper, best, and most pleasant for him: he must live a life of reason.

Aristotle reminds the student of ethics that the gods are considered to be happy and blessed. Yet no one supposes that the gods are happy because of being just, brave, or temperate. The value of divine existence comes from activity superior to that devoted to practical action and production; the happiness of the gods consists in the activity of contemplation.

Aristotle admits that to be happy a man must be prosperous enough to sustain himself as a healthy and active person. But moderate advantages and temperate practices are enough to make a happy life possible.

The laws are important, claims Aristotle, because they force human beings, particularly the young, into habits which encourage and exemplify the good life. No man is made good merely by nature or by teaching, and the right habits will be developed only if legislators are directed by an appreciation of whatever is noble and virtuous. The art of politics is involved in the attempt to secure the conditions which make virtuous living possible.

Happiness is the highest good, then, according to Aristotle, but it is the happiness of the man who, exercising the faculty peculiar to him—a faculty which represents the best that is in him—is actively contemplative. Aristotle's ethics is a challenge to man; it calls upon him to exceed himself and thereby to attain happiness:

If reason is divine, then, in comparison with man, the life according to it is divine in comparison with human life. But we must not follow those who advise us, being men, to think of human things, and, being mortal, of mortal things, but must, so far as we can, make ourselves immortal, and strain every nerve to live in accordance with the best thing in us; for even if it be small in bulk, much more does it in power and worth surpass everything . . . . And what we said before will apply now; that which is proper to each thing is by nature best and most pleasant for each thing; for man, therefore, the life according to reason is best and pleasantest, since reason more than anything else *is* man. This life therefore is also the happiest.

IV

～☞☜～

EPICURUS: THE
GOOD AS PLEASURE

Although both Plato and Aristotle were inclined to regard the virtuous life as a pleasant one, neither supposed pleasure to be the only thing worthwhile on its own account or that a man's life ought to be devoted to securing a balance of pleasure over pain. However, the Greek philosopher Epicurus (c.342-c.270 B.C.), who was about twenty years old at the time of Aristotle's death, built his entire ethics around the claim that pleasure is the only thing good as an end—and pain the only thing that in itself is bad. For practical reasons Epicurus tended to regard the most pleasant life as one enjoyed by a man who, limiting his desires to what is necessary and possible, makes prudence his central virtue, and makes the avoidance of pain a more important consideration than the active pursuit of pleasure. The peace of mind and body secured by one who lives a quiet and moderate life is conducive to a pleasant state of mind which Epicurus called *ataraxia*, "contentment" or "serenity." Most of Epicurus's ethics is taken up with advice concerning the attainment of *ataraxia*.

The three principal sources of Epicurus's ethical views are his *Letter to Menoeceus*, the *Principal Doctrines*, and the account given in Lucretius's *De Rerum Natura* (On the Nature of Things). The two former sources, both very brief, were incorporated in the biography

43

of Epicurus by Diogenes Laertius (as part of Diogenes's *Lives and Opinions of Eminent Philosophers*, written sometime in the second or third century A.D.).

Epicurus was an atomistic materialist; he believed that everything is either atoms or empty space. It is not surprising, then, that he was influenced not by religious or metaphysical views, but by those Platonic arguments in which the value of the pleasures of this world was emphasized, as well as by the hedonistic (pleasure-centered) philosophy of the Cyrenaic philosopher Aristippus, who argued that the goal of life is the enjoyment of the most immediate and intense pleasures. But Epicurus's ethics is distinguishable from that of Plato by its view of justice as a political arrangement for mutual advantage, and by its exclusive emphasis on pleasure and the avoidance of pain. And Epicurus's philosophy of morality differs from that of Aristippus in that Epicurus rejected Aristippus's emphasis on the pleasure of the present moment—to be attained through gratification of the sensual appetites—in favor of a philosophy recommending the modest pleasures of contemplation, restraint, and friendship.

"Death is nothing to us . . . ."

The atomism of Epicurus led him to warn men about the dangers to peace of mind that come from taking religious superstitions seriously and from holding false opinions about death. He did not deny that there are gods, but he insisted that "they are not such as the many believe them to be . . . ." Experience shows that men ought not to count on the gods for the rewards of a virtuous life, and hence Epicurus describes the good man as one who, although holding that the proper attitude towards the gods is one of reverence, nevertheless "thinks that with us lies the chief power of determining events . . . ."

As for death, Epicurus has this to say:

Become accustomed to the belief that death is nothing to us. For all good and evil consists in sensation, but death is deprivation of sensation. And therefore a right understanding that death is nothing to us makes the mortality of life enjoyable, not because it adds to it an infinite span of time, but because it takes away the craving for immortality. For there is nothing terrible in life for the man who has truly comprehended that there is nothing terrible in not living. So that the man speaks but idly who says that he fears death not because it will be painful when it comes, but because it is painful in anticipation. For that which gives no trouble when it comes, is but an empty pain in anticipation. So death, the most terrifying of ills, is nothing to us, since so long as we exist death is not with us; but when death comes, then we do not exist. It does not then concern either the living or the dead, since for the former it is not, and the latter are no more.

This persuasive argument, taken from the *Letter to Menoeceus*, is echoed in the *Principal Doctrines* (a collection of epigrams), when Epicurus writes: "Death is nothing to us; for that which is dissolved is without sensation; and that which lacks sensation is nothing to us."

Epicurus stressed the point that fear is usually the result of ignorance. Those who allow the fear of the gods and of death to master them have not taken advantage of the findings of the natural sciences: "If we were not troubled by our suspicions of the phenomena of the sky and about death, fearing that it concerns us, and also by our failure to grasp the limits of pains and desires, we should have no need of natural science" (*Principal Doctrines*, XI). And again, "A man cannot dispel his fear about the most important matters if he does not know what is the nature of the universe but suspects the truth of some mythical story. So that without natural science it is not possible to attain our pleasures unalloyed" (*Principal Doctrines*, XII).

Not only the natural sciences but also philosophy is necessary if a man is to overcome the fears that result from ignorance. A memorable passage on the value of philosophy introduces the *Letter to Menoeceus*:

Let no one when young delay to study philosophy, nor when he is old grow weary of his study. For no one can come too early or too late to secure the health of his soul. And the man who says that the age for philosophy has either not yet come or has gone by is like the man who says that the age for happiness is not yet come to him, or has passed away. Wherefore both when young and old a man must study philosophy, that as he grows old he may be young in blessings through the grateful recollection of what has been, and that in youth he may be old as well, since he will know no fear of what is to come. We must then meditate on the things that make our happiness, seeing that when that is with us we have all, but when it is absent we do all to win it.

Pleasure and the good life

Having counseled Menoeceus to the effect that happiness depends upon ridding oneself of fears about the gods and death, Epicurus refers to various kinds of desires and discusses their relation to the problem of securing happiness and the health of the soul. He argues that some desires are "natural," others are "vain"; "and of the natural some are necessary and other merely natural; and of the necessary some are necessary for happiness, others for the repose of the body, and others for very life." An understanding of these differences among desires is important, writes Epicurus, because the happy life, "the life of blessedness," depends upon making the right choices for "the health of the body and the soul's freedom from disturbance . . . ." If only man can avoid pain and fear, Epicurus assures Menoeceus, pleasure will follow; and it is for the sake of pleasure, "the first good innate in us," that men choose some things and avoid others. Every good is judged by reference to the feeling of pleasure.

Epicurus argues that not every pleasure is to be chosen, for some pleasures (pleasant activities) eventually lead to greater discomfort than others do. In deciding what to do, a man must consider the advantages and disadvantages—that is, the degree to which what he does will yield pain or displeasure. Epicurus's firm conclusion is that "it is not continuous drinkings and revellings, nor the satisfaction of lusts, nor the enjoyment of fish and other luxuries of the wealthy table, which produce a pleasant life, but sober reasoning, searching out the motives for all choice and avoidance . . . ."

What Epicurus calls "sober reasoning"—that is, the careful calculation of consequences by reference to pleasures and pains—must be supplemented, if one is to lead the good life, by right opinion. Epicurus declares that "mere opinions"—by which he means opinions without the support provided by experience—bring about "the greatest disturbance of the spirit." The virtuous man, then, is "he who holds reverent opinions concerning the gods, and is at all times free from fear of death, and has reasoned out the end ordained by nature . . . ." Far from succumbing to the self-defeating desires of the profligate who hopes that chance events will favor him, the prudent (and, consequently, happy) man "thinks it better to be unfortunate in reasonable action than to prosper in unreason. For it is better in a man's actions that what is well chosen should fail,

rather than what is ill chosen should be successful owing to chance."
Epicurus is careful to emphasize his claim that pleasure itself is
never bad, but activities that disturb a man's quiet appreciation of
the freedom from fear and ignorance are wrong because of the displeasure that accompanies them. "No pleasure is a bad thing in
itself," he writes in the *Principal Doctrines*,"but the means which
produce some pleasures bring with them disturbances many times
greater than the pleasures." Again, he writes, "If the things that
produce the pleasures of profligates could dispel the fears of the
mind about the phenomena of the sky and death and its pains, and
also teach the limits of desires and of pains, we should never have
cause to blame them . . . ."

The greatest moral good, then is prudence. Epicurus insists that a
pleasant life is not possible if it is not a prudent and honorable life.
So close is the relationship between virtue and pleasure that it is not
possible to have the one without the other: ". . . the virtues are by
nature bound up with the pleasant life, and the pleasant life is insep-
arable from them" (*Letter to Menoeceus*). And in the *Principal Doctrines*: "It is not possible to live pleasantly without living prudently
and honourably and justly, nor again to live a life of prudence,
honour, and justice without living pleasantly."

According to Epicurus, the prudent life is a quiet one, a life in
which the desire for fame and frenetic public activity has no part:
"The most unalloyed source of protection from men, which is secured to some extent by a certain force of expulsion, is in fact the
immunity which results from a quiet life and the retirement from
the world." Epicurus's advice is to avoid giving in to the desire to
become "famous and conspicuous"; by far the better course is to
"live unknown," enjoying the peace of mind that comes from stay-
ing within "the limits of life . . . ."

For Epicurus, as for Plato and Aristotle, friendship is a primary
source of satisfaction for the virtuous man. "Of all the things which
wisdom acquires to produce the blessedness of the complete life, far
the greatest is the possession of friendship," he writes (*Principal
Doctrines*, XXVII). Fragments of the philosopher's writings (from
the *Vatican Collection*) testify to the value of friendship: "All
friendship is desirable in itself, though it starts from the need of
help," and, "Friendship goes dancing round the world proclaiming
to us all to awake to the praises of a happy life."

In his *Life of Epicurus*, Diogenes Laertius reports that, according to Epicurus, "friendship . . . has practical needs as its motive: one must indeed lay its foundations (for we sow the ground too for the sake of crops), but it is formed and maintained by means of community of life among those who have reached the fullness of pleasure."

Justice and mutual advantage

The importance of the community is emphasized in Epicurus's account of justice. The view of justice is naturalistic, not metaphysical (as one might expect from a philosopher who, maintaining that everything is understandable in terms of atoms and void, described the soul as "a body of fine particles . . . most resembling wind with a certain admixture of heat . . ."). "The justice which arises from nature," he writes, "is a pledge of mutual advantage to restrain men from harming one another and save them from being harmed." There is no justice (or injustice) for those who have not made "compacts not to harm one another or be harmed . . . ."

Unlike those philosophers who regard injustice (or the condition of one who has acted wrongly) as intrinsically evil, Epicurus took a practical view of the matter: "Injustice is not an evil in itself, but only in consequence of the fear which attaches to the apprehension of being unable to escape those appointed to punish such actions."

Although Epicurus regarded justice as relative to the laws or agreements made by men, he distinguished between good laws and bad ones by reference to the mutual advantage to be secured through a law that is just. Laws, he declares, "are no longer just, when no longer of advantage."

It is apparent from a study of the extant writings of Epicurus that the ethical philosophy there expressed is quite different in content and spirit from that commonly associated with the term "Epicurean." Although Epicurus regarded bodily pleasure as the only good and pain as the only evil, he distinguished between those pleasures we call "sensual" and those we call "intellectual" or "rational." He maintained that the latter pleasures are preferable to the former because of the circumstantial advantages of a life governed by reason, disciplined by experience, and limited to what is within the range of man's powers. Not the active pursuit of pleasure, but the avoidance of fear, ignorance, and the desire for what is unattainable or unprofitable (in terms of the pleasures and pains), was set forth as a program for the man who would be virtuous and, hence, happy.

V

EPICTETUS: THE
GOOD LIFE AS IN
ACCORD WITH NATURE

Epicurus and his followers believed in achieving happiness through avoiding the pains of ignorance and harmful desire, and consequently they urged men to live moderately, to rid their minds of superstitions, and to perfect the art of choosing wisely by avoiding the temptation to seek the pleasures of the moment. Epictetus and his fellow Stoics, by contrast, were disdainful of the effort to achieve happiness through the avoidance of painful or unpleasant activity. The Stoics believed in accepting with deliberate equanimity anything that might come—pleasant or unpleasant, painful or not. According to the Stoics, one cannot manipulate the ways of the world; the secret of happiness, then, is a proud tolerance of whatever may be a man's fortune, be it good or bad. A man's primary responsibility, if he is to lead the good life, is to distinguish between what is in his power and what is not, and then to confine himself to the former.

The Stoic philosopher Epictetus (c. 65–c. 135) represents a late and sophisticated development of a line of thought that began with the Cynics of the early fourth century B.C. Cynics such as Antisthenes and Diogenes maintained that conventional ways of life are destructive and dishonest; the only good and honest way to live is in accordance with nature. Hence, the Cynics adopted simple, coarse clothing, and they lived like beggars. Antisthenes and Diogenes (the latter famous as the lantern-bearer who walked about in broad daylight looking for an honest man) believed in achieving complete independence of spirit through freeing themselves from any dependency on external possessions or events. They regarded virtue as its own reward, and virtue was defined as any mode of life that liberates a man from convention and allows him to live naturally.

Predecessors of Epictetus

The first Stoic was Zeno of Citium (who died about 260 B.C., not to be confused with the master of paradoxes, Zeno of Elea, who lived in the fifth century B.C.). Zeno, born in Cyprus, lived and taught in Athens, and made his philosophical headquarters in a collonaded portico, the *Stoa Poikile* (Painted Porch), from which the school derived its name. Zeno emphasized the value of a life lived in accord with nature (and in doing so reflected his study under the Cynics). Like Socrates, Zeno taught that death is no evil, although the reason he gave was not that the soul is immaterial, but that "there are cases of a glorious death," a consideration that is characteristically Stoic. He regarded the soul as body, arguing that the soul, when ashamed, turns the body red. But his materialism worked both ways: the soul may be body, but the universe itself has feelings and is a living thing. Zeno tended to identify the good with being itself.

Cleanthes, Zeno's successor as the head of the Stoic school, transformed Stoicism, at least during the time of his leadership, from a philosophical emphasis on ethics, physics, and logic into a religion. His *Hymn to Zeus* expresses a theology which presents God as the source of order and unity, the "One Word" and source of universal law. Knowledge of God's "Word" or law, which is the law of all nature, is what makes men rational and happy.

Chrysippus, a pupil of Cleanthes, restored the earlier Stoic emphasis on learning and the art of argumentation. The doctrine of the Old Stoa emphasized the value of "apathy"—an indifference or calmness despite the turns of fate. The justification of apathy was a rational one: insofar as the universe is one, it is good; and insofar as its course is not to be altered, the rational and virtuous attitude is one of acceptance through understanding and a strong will.

A great deal of the ingenuity of the early Stoics was spent in the effort to show that accepting the natural course of events is both rational and virtuous. Many men suppose that they see evil in destructive events, but that is because their understanding is partial. If a man once recognizes that everything that happens is part of the whole, and if he sees that it is his own attitude that endows natural events with evil, he can overcome his passionate tendency to reject what is probably not only inevitable but also good and divine.

The principal Stoics of the period before the emergence of Roman Stoicism were Diogenes of Seleucia (*not* Diogenes the Cynic, who was born about 412 B.C., 200 years earlier), Panaetius (born c. 190 B.C.), and Poseidonius (born c.135 B.C.). Under their leadership, the Stoic school emphasized the natural sciences and some of the principal theses of Platonic philosophy.

Roman Stoicism involved a development of earlier Greek views, but its distinctive character and appeal derived from the persuasive power of independent Roman thinkers, principally Seneca (c. 4 B.C.–A.D. 65), Epictetus (c. 65–c. 135), and Marcus Aurelius (121–180). Seneca was a wealthy business man and politician, whose Stoical writings were more concerned with problems of ethics than with logic and metaphysics. Epictetus was a well-educated slave, born a Phrygian, who established himself as one of the most influential philosophers of his period. His work is important as representing a deliberate effort to work out the ethical implications of early Stoicism and it had a profound influence on the thinking of the emperor Marcus Aurelius, whose *Meditations'* is primarily a reflective and didactic (although self-instructive) restatement of views developed by Epictetus.

The *Discourses* of Epictetus are lecture notes compiled by one of his students, Arrian. The transcription is apparently so accurate and complete that the work may be regarded as an authentic expression of Epictetus's ideas.

The right use of impressions

Epictetus begins by emphasizing that "the power to deal rightly with our impressions" is a gift of the gods. He speaks of Zeus as saying that since the god could not make the body, which is but clay, "free and untrammelled," he gave to man "a portion in our divinity, this faculty of impulse to act and not to act, of will to get and will to avoid, in a word the faculty which can turn impressions to right use."

Education is necessary, says Epictetus, in order that men learn to adjust their ideas of what is rational and irrational so as to bring themselves into harmony with nature. Epictetus points out that "rational and irrational mean different things to different persons, just as good and evil, expedient and inexpedient, are different for different persons." If a man is to decide whether he is being true to himself if he performs a lowly service for another in order to avoid a beating, he must first know himself, and only then will he be in a position to know at what price he will sell himself.

In appraising himself, Epictetus advises, a man should remember that men are all "children of God and that God is the Father of gods and men . . . ." Those who remember only their animal bodies tend to become like beasts, but those who realize that they share their minds and power of reason with the gods are thereby strengthened in their effort to make rational uses of their impressions.

Moral progress does not come simply, as through the reading of the works of Chrysippus, but only through discipline of the will, Epictetus argues. A man who wills to avoid what is unavoidable will never know peace of mind. To be in harmony with nature, a man must know the limits of his own power, and his will must operate within those limits.

The rationality of nature

There are those who question the ways of Providence, however, and to them Epictetus addresses himself in no uncertain terms: "Each single thing that comes into being in the universe affords a ready ground for praising Providence, if one possesses these two qualities—a power to see clearly the circumstances of each, and the spirit of gratitude therewith." Epictetus develops an argument by design, pointing out the analogy between the products of human craftsmen and natural objects adapted for their functions. Man's power of reason is evidence of God's intention that men understand the rationality of nature and that they govern themselves accordingly. If men understand that their rationality is derived from God, they will realize that each man is "a citizen of the universe" and "a son of God." The recognition of man's kinship with God enables man to see that although death is no evil and the body is nothing in comparison with the spirit, each man is obligated to perform the service in life which God has appointed him to serve. No man, then should take his own life, for to do so would be to depart life without having a justifiable reason such as would be afforded were God to give the signal (through a natural death).

Having urged that men recognize the rationality of nature, Epictetus draws this moral: "When a man has his proper station in life, he does not hanker after what is beyond him." Epictetus imagines someone declaring, "I am content if I am in accord with Nature in what I will to get and will to avoid, if I follow Nature in impulse to act and to refrain from action, in purpose, and design and assent." Epictetus then points out that anyone who intends to follow nature, both in his impulses to act and in his refraining from action, should not concern himself with winning the admiration of men whose views of man's station in life are quite different from his own.

The principle of living which Epictetus urges is explicitly set forth as "the law of life": "But . . . the law of living . . . is this–to act in conformity with nature. For if we wish in every subject and in all circumstances to observe what is natural, it is plain that in everything we must aim at not letting slip what is in harmony with nature nor accepting what is in conflict with it."

Epictetus explains that the problem of living harmoniously with nature involves three distinct efforts on man's part: the effort to understand the course of nature, the effort to recognize the limits of one's own faculties, and the effort to relate action to the knowledge of nature and of one's self.

Good and evil as dependent on will

The problem of what one ought to do in life can be resolved only by considering what is good and evil. But good and evil, although dependent for their "material" on what is external to man, are dependent for their status as values on man's will. "The essence of good and of evil lies in an attitude of the will," he writes. External things, however, are but "materials for the will, in dealing with which it will find its own good or evil."

According to Epictetus, then, the central problem of morality is not that of deciding when the general or primary conceptions of value and obligation apply to particular cases. He suggests that everyone knows "that the good is expedient and desirable and that we ought in all circumstances to follow and pursue it . . . ." But conflict of opinion arises "in the application of primary conceptions to particular facts; when for instance one says, 'He has done well: he is brave,' and another, 'Nay, he is out of his mind.' "

For one who recognizes the power of the will, such matters as exile, death, prison, dishonor, and condemnation are "indifferent." Anything, whether pleasant or painful, is indifferent which lies outside the mind's control. The paradox of morality is that the good man shows both confidence and caution at the same time: confidence with regard to matters beyond the will, and caution concerning things which depend on the will.

The views of Epicurus come under attack by Epictetus. Epicurus is charged with claiming that there is no natural fellowship of rational beings, while Epictetus insists that what distinguishes men from the beasts is their recognition of the primacy of will and of the importance of knowledge as providing material for the rational control of life. If the good be nothing but pleasure, as Epicurus argues, then, says Epictetus in reply, ". . .be off with you and go to sleep; do as the worm does, for this is the life of which you pronounce yourself worthy: eating, drinking, copulation, evacuation, and snoring." Epictetus suggests bitterly that Epicurus is perfectly willing to corrupt young men with his views, while Epicurus himself submits himself to the painful discipline of writing books for the good of others. "What, then, was it that roused Epicurus from his slumbers and compelled him to write what he wrote?" asks Epictetus. And he provides a firm answer: "What else but that which is the most powerful of all human things, Nature, which draws a man to her will though he groan and resist?"

Knowledge as sufficient to virtue

Epictetus is sympathetic with the Socratic idea that knowledge is sufficient to virtue. A man who errs is acting against what he wishes, since he wishes to do the right thing. So long as a man acts in ignorance of the degree to which what he is doing is opposed to his interest, he will persist, but once he can be shown that either he is not doing what he wishes, or is doing what he does not wish, "strong necessity makes him abandon the conflict" (between action and the will). Epictetus remarks that "Socrates knew what moves the rational soul, and that it will incline to what moves it, whether it wishes to or not. Show the conflict to the rational Governing Principle and he will desist. If you do not show it, blame yourself rather than him who refuses to obey."

Having discussed the basic tenets of his ethics, Epictetus applies the general principles to various kinds of moral problems. He comments on the hair arrangement and dress of a student, and suggests that the beauty of the self is more important than outward appearance. There is a kind of beauty appropriate to each kind of animal, and man's beauty consists in an ordering of the will and of the power of judgment.

Epictetus then criticizes the Procurator of Epirus for having "offended decorum by the way he showed interest in a comedian . . . ." Epictetus chides the Procurator for objecting to the excitable reviling of the crowd—if the Procurator cannot himself keep calm in the theatre, how can he expect others to behave properly?

He criticizes those who offer illness as an excuse for leaving a lecture-room, and contends that if a serious interest were taken in the improvement of the will through bringing one's "Governing Principle . . . into accord with nature," the student would not be so eager to rush home to his nice bed. Epictetus's bitterness is evident: "Go to your mother then; for you deserve to be ill, with her to hold your head . . . . Go to your nice bed then; sick or well you deserve to lie on a bed of that sort!"

Action within one's power

Epictetus has Stoical advice for those who get bad news, for those who would be teachers or philosophers, for those who fail to reach some objective they have set for themselves, for those who cannot bear to be pitied, for someone formerly modest who has become shameless—in short, Epictetus has practical moral advice for men of all sorts, and his advice is directed by the fundamental ideas that a man should limit his efforts to what is within his power, and should be guided by his reason and in the knowledge that all men are the children of God.

The *Manual* of Epictetus, compiled by Arrian, although very short, is useful as a summary of the basic principles brought out in the teaching of Epictetus. The first idea emphasized is the fundamental Stoic precept that a distinction must be made between what is in our power and what is not. Those who try to avoid death, disease, and poverty will probably be miserable, while those who seek control of their wills and then give more than ordinary effort to the attainment of what is within their power will probably be happy.

Control of the will is important, but right living demands knowledge not only of what is within one's power but also of the nature of things. Epictetus's advice is clear:

When anything, from the meanest thing upwards, is attractive or serviceable or an object of affection, remember always to say to yourself, "What is its nature?" If you are fond of a jug, say you are fond of a jug; then you will not be disturbed if it be broken. If you kiss your child or your wife, say to yourself that you are kissing a human being, for then if death strikes it you will not be disturbed.

The central Stoical precept is summarized in a fashion that makes the injunction memorable: "Ask not that events should happen as you will, but let your will be that events should happen as they do, and you shall have peace." Such an injunction, however, is useless unless it is supplemented by the reminder that man has the power, provided that he exercises it within the range of effectiveness, to affect the course of events. "When anything happens to you, always remember to turn to yourself and ask what faculty you have to deal with it."

Perhaps Epictetus found that obeying the course of nature was no guarantee of satisfying the practical demands laid on a man by other men. "If you wish to make progress," the *Manual* represents Epictetus as advising, "you must be content in external matters to seem a fool and a simpleton." What follows is somewhat poignant, perhaps because it rings true: "For know that it is not easy to keep your will in accord with nature and at the same time keep outward things; if you attend to one you must needs neglect the other."

There is an element of fatalism in the ethics of Epictetus; the course of nature is directed by a greater will than man's: "Remember that you are an actor in a play, and the Playwright chooses the manner of it: if he wants it short, it is short; if long, it is long."

Epictetus emphasizes repeatedly that nature is not in itself bad or evil; it is in man's response to nature and in his judgment of the course of nature that evil comes into being. "What disturbs men's minds is not events but their judgments on events," we read. And, again, "Remember that foul words or blows in themselves are no outrage, but your judgment that they are so." And, finally: "As a mark is not set up for men to miss it, so there is nothing intrinsically evil in the world."

Charity toward others

Something like charity is urged as a moral virtue in passages in which Epictetus is represented as asking those who would pass judgment on others to consider that every man, when he acts, does what he thinks is fitting for him. The Socratic idea that the man who errs in his opinion suffers from self-deception is endorsed as an idea that encourages a man, even when reviled by another, to "be gentle to him who reviles you, saying to yourself on each occasion, 'He thought it right.' " Epictetus warns against pride. Preoccupation with oneself and one's powers distracts a man from the serious business of life, which is to understand, to keep control of one's impressions, to exercise the will rationally, and to direct oneself only to what is within one's power. Socrates attained perfection, according to Epictetus, because Socrates paid heed only to reason. "And if you are not yet Socrates, yet ought you to live as one who would wish to be Socrates."

Stoicism is sometimes represented as the view that the highest virtue is that of bearing up under the agonies of existence. But although Epictetus, as well as other Stoics, urged that men not complain or grieve about the unavoidable turns of fortune, he also emphasized the possibilities of creative and compassionate action within the limits of power which nature leaves for men. Epictetus says, with Cleanthes, "Lead me, O Zeus, and lead me, Destiny,/Whither ordained is by your decree." And with Euripides he declares, "Who rightly with necessity complies/ In things divine we count him skilled and wise." But at the same time he asks, "How long will you wait to think yourself worthy of the highest and transgress in nothing the clear pronouncement of reason?" And he sternly enjoins, as a Socratic moral principle, the following general directive: ". . . make up your mind before it is too late to live as one who is mature and proficient, and let all that seems best to you be a law that you cannot transgress." To live by such a moral imperative takes courage, but to conceive of the imperative and to order one's impressions so that one's course of action is effective in securing what is highest and best takes a resourceful combination of a clear eye, a sense of reason, and a constant piety. As Epictetus conceived him, the Stoic is not a long-suffering brute, but a whole man, courageous, sensitive, rational, and eminently practical.

VI

~~~~~~

HUME: MORALITY
AS DETERMINED
BY SENTIMENT

In his *Enquiry Concerning the Principles of Morals*, David Hume (1711–1776) declares as his objective an examination of the question as to whether the foundations of morals are derived from reason or from sentiment. He comments that despite the confusion that discussion of this problem has provoked, arguments on both sides tend to have a certain persuasive power; and he recognizes the possibility that both reason and sentiment are involved in moral judgment. His inquiry is designed to clarify the matter so as to make the "true origin of morals" apparent; it can then be decided how reason and sentiment relate to moral considerations.

Hume's conclusion is "that morality is determined by sentiment," and virtue is "whatever mental action or quality gives to a spectator the pleasant sentiment of approbation." Whenever a moral judgment is made (if it is made responsibly), all the circumstances relating to conduct have to be determined and considered; then sentiment—"approbation or blame"—settles the matter. First there must be *knowledge* of the matter to be judged; then *feeling* provides the sentiment on the basis of which a value judgment can be made. Ultimate ends are not decided upon by the use of reason, but according to "sentiments and affections."

The emphasis in Hume's ethics upon feeling or sentiment has led many critics to describe Hume as anticipating the influential twentieth-century view that moral judgments are nothing more than emotive expressions, sometimes used in the effort to encourage a certain line of conduct. (See the discussion of A. J. Ayer's position, Chapter X.) But Hume's philosophy of morality is clearly different from later emotive accounts in that while philosophers like Ayer and Charles L. Stevenson concentrate on the emotive functions of value terms, Hume insisted upon the determination of matters of fact as prerequisite to a knowledgeable survey that gives rise to the emotional attitude which finally makes a value or moral judgment possible. Thus Hume writes, "In moral decisions, *all the circumstances and relations must be previously known*; and the mind, from the contemplation of the whole, *feels* some new impression of affection or disgust, esteem or contempt, approbation or blame." (Italics added.) Again, "Before we can pretend to form any decision of this kind [that is, a moral decision], *everything must be known and ascertained* on the side of the object or action. Nothing remains but to feel, on our part, some sentiment of blame or approbation; whence we pronounce the action criminal or virtuous." (Italics added.)

Benevolence and justice

Hume's enquiry begins with an examination of the "social virtues"–benevolence and justice. He first of all remarks that the traits of character designated by such terms as "humane," "merciful," "generous," "beneficent," and "sociable" are universally prized as representing the "highest merit, which *human nature* is capable of attaining." These social virtues, says Hume, "engage every heart, on the first apprehension of them . . . ."

And it is, in fact, the engagement of the heart on the apprehension of character that entitles us to conclude that such traits are worthwhile. Hume's theory of value is thus implicit even at the outset of the *Enquiry*.

At least part of the merit of benevolence lies in its utility, Hume decides after an examination of the circumstances of judgment. Practices originally approved of because of their presumed utility in serving the interests of society are disapproved of once it is discovered that the practice does more harm than good. "In all determinations of morality," writes Hume, "this circumstance of public utility is ever principally in view . . . ." The benevolent man wins approval because by his acts he contributes to the happiness of men and to the satisfaction of social concerns.

However, men are favorably disposed toward benevolence not only because of its social utility, but also because of its "softness and tenderness" as a sentiment. It is enjoyable to know, through sympathy, the feelings of love and friendship which animate the generous and benevolent man. There are certain qualities of character, then, according to Hume, which are immdediately agreeable; and they are so because the person who has the qualities associated with benevolence delights in them, and by sympathy his delight affects others and leads them to look with approval on the benevolent man.

Turning to a consideration of the appeal of justice, Hume argues that men approve of justice (by which he means the proper distribution of private property) solely because of its public utility. In a community in which all needs and interests were met and satisfied, justice would be useless and, consequently, without merit. From the Humean point of view, unless a way of acting gives rise to "the pleasing sentiment of approbation," it cannot be a virtue. "The necessity of justice to the support of society is the sole foundation of that virtue," Hume contends. Since both benevolence and justice are esteemed because of their utility (and justice *only* because of its utility), the usefulness of a mode of action or trait of character is probably the most important factor influencing moral sentiment.

Hume maintains that laws are worthwhile only insofar as they are useful, and political society—or government—is regarded with approval only because of its utility. If men were by nature wise and generous, there would be no need for government and its laws. Since there is clearly an advantage to be gained from regulating society, however, men give their approval to political order, and duties—rights and wrongs—are thereby established.

The appeal of utility

Hume considers the problem of accounting for utility's appeal. He quickly disposes of the suggestion that the moral sentiment in favor of utility is the product of politically controlled education. The appeal of utility must rest in some natural circumstance that gives meaning to the language of politicians.

Hume also rejects the idea that social utility is approved because each man, moved by self-love, supposes that whatever is useful for the community as fostering order and the general welfare is also useful for him personally. He points out that men often look favorably upon acts remote in time or space, without stopping to consider whether such acts in any way benefit them as individuals. Nor do we, through the imagination, enjoy useful acts as if they were useful for us even when they are not. Hume's conclusion is that "we must renounce the theory, which accounts for every moral sentiment by the principle of self-love."

Having begun his enquiry into the appeal of utility by presupposing a reason for the approbation of useful acts, Hume finds himself, after examination of the problem, driven to conclude that "everything which contributes to the happiness of society recommends itself directly to our approbation and good-will." The principle of benevolence, then, is fundamental; it does not itself need a defense, for it has a natural origin. "It appears to be matter of fact," Hume writes, "that the circumstance of *utility*, in all subjects, is a source of praise and approbation: That it is constantly appealed to in all moral decisions concerning the merit and demerit of actions . . . that it is a foundation of the chief part of morals, which has a reference to mankind and our fellow-creatures."

Hume takes note of the Aristotelean idea that virtue is constituted by the mean between excesses, but he argues that the "due medium" is determined primarily by the advantages, or utility, of a "quality" of character. In fact, as he later points out in his conclusion, excesses are themselves determined by reference to the damage done by certain kinds of conduct. Hume argues that it is pointless to argue that temperance is better than excesses, "when it appears that these excesses are only denominated such, because they are hurtful . . . ."

Character traits or qualities, then, are neither absolutely blameable nor absolutely praiseworthy, but the value of any personal quality is dependent upon the degree to which that quality is useful to the person whose quality it is. Hume also argues that advantageous qualities in another are agreeable to those who contemplate him, not because by self-love the spectator places himself in the position of the other, but because the natural sentiments of sympathy and humanity show themselves as pleasure in the contemplation of another's success in his undertakings.

Among the qualities "useful to ourselves" are "discretion, caution, enterprise, industry, assiduity, frugality, economy, good-sense, prudence, discernment . . . ." In addition to these, Hume mentions the following qualities: "Temperance, sobriety, patience, constancy, perseverance, forethought, considerateness, secrecy, order, insinuation, address, presence of mind, quickness of conception, facility of expression . . . ." In every case, Hume contends, the value of virtues "consists in their tendency to serve the person . . . ."

Again, in considering the value of certain "bodily endowments," Hume finds that the main source of approbation of such features as broad shoulders, "firm joints, taper legs," derives from their utility. A man capable of success in battle or in the ordinary enterprises of life tends to win approval for the features that he has and is, accordingly, said to be handsome.

Immediately agreeable qualities

Certain traits of character are immediately agreeable to ourselves, Hume contends, while other qualities are immediately agreeable to others. Since virtue is defined as "a quality of the mind agreeable to or approved of by everyone who considers or contemplates it," and since although some virtues are approved because of their utility, others are approved on sight—"immediately"—a consideration of the latter class of virtues is relevant to ethics.

A person who enjoys his own qualities—his own cheerfulness, serenity, or poetic talent—tends to arouse agreeable sentiments in others. The reason why some qualities, whatever their utility, are "immediately" agreeable is that the person who has them is himself pleased, and others then "enter into the same humour, and catch the sentiment, by a contagion or natural sympathy . . . ." Even benevolence, a social virtue with an obvious ground in utility, is to some degree capable of being immediately agreeable, for the benevolent man is generally happy in his benevolence, and the delight he enjoys is communicated to others.

The "attentions and regards" by which we conduct ourselves in the company of others, Hume writes, are also immediately agreeable. Good manners are appealing quite apart from any consideration of their utility. Wit and the ability to converse in a lively and interesting way are also qualities agreeable to others. Other immediately agreeable virtues include modesty, self-confidence, decency ("a proper regard to age, sex, character, and station in the world"), cleanliness, and finally, "something mysterious and inexplicable"—a man's personal manner or style, "an ease, a genteelness, and I-know-not-what, which some men possess above others . . . ."

In his conclusion, Hume expresses surprise that the theory of value he has advanced was not discovered by the first philosophers of morality. "Whatever is valuable in any kind," he writes, ". . . naturally classes itself under the division of *useful* or *agreeable* . . . ," and consequently personal merit, or value as a person, "consists altogether in the possession of mental qualities, *useful* or *agreeable* to the *person himself* or to *others*."

If one now puts the monkish "virtues" of "celibacy, fasting, penance, mortification, self-denial, humility, silence, solitude" to the test, we find reason, Hume argues, for deciding that these qualities belong in the list of vices, for ". . . they [are] everywhere rejected by men of sense, . . . they serve to no manner of purpose; neither advance a man's fortune in the world, nor render him a more valuable member of society; neither qualify him for the entertainment of company, nor increase his power of self-enjoyment . . . ."

Hume refuses to be drawn into controversy concerning the amount of benevolence or self-love in human nature. He argues that it is enough to realize that every man has something of both sentiments, and since morality depends on some common sentiment that moves all men to agree in their judgments, an ethics which points out the universality of the sentiment of humanity (general benevolence) fulfils its obligation as a philosophical examination of morality. The sentiment of self-love is not as common and comprehensive as the sentiment of benevolence, Hume contends, for self-love is felt in different ways and does not encompass all men as objects of its concern. Humanity (the sentiment of benevolence), on the other hand, yields sentiments that "are not only the same in all human creatures, and produce the same approbation or censure; but they also comprehend all human creatures; nor is there any one whose conduct or character is not, by their means, an object to everyone of censure or approbation."

Even if Hume's postulation of the sentiments of humanity and sympathy is denied, the claim that virtue consists in whatever quality of mind is useful or agreeable to the person himself or to others survives, Hume insists, for such qualities give pleasure to anyone who contemplates them and hence win approval.

Virtue and moral obligation

Hume briefly considers the relation of virtue to moral obligation. He suggests that an ethics which portrays virtue as aiming at making

all men cheerful and happy, rather than calling for "useless auster-
ities and rigours, suffering and self-denial," has already gone a long
way toward making the practice of virtue a matter of duty. "The
sole trouble which she [virtue] demands," he writes, "is that of just
calculation, and a steady preference of the greater happiness." If
what a man secures by his action is something useful or agreeable to
himself, he is quite naturally drawn to it; if what he secures is useful
or agreeable to others, he is nevertheless encouraged in his action by
the feeling of benevolence, which is "sweet, smooth, tender, and
agreeable, independent of all fortune and accidents."

Hume becomes something of a moralist in his response to the
question of a possible conflict between self-interest and moral obligation. He concedes that although it is generally true, that, for example, honesty is the best policy, there are exceptions to that rule. And
he concedes also that those who are tempted to take advantage of
the exceptions may be beyond the reach of any moral appeal. Unless
the "heart rebel" against pernicious reasoning and practices, there is
no motive to virtue. But Hume reminds those who are tempted to
give self-interest priority in the violation of moral rules that "the
unbought satisfaction of conversation, society, study, even health
and the common beauties of nature, but above all the peaceful reflection on one's own conduct . . ." are pleasures far superior to "the
feverish, empty amusements of luxury and expense."

In the first appendix to the *Enquiry*, Hume returns to the original
question—that of deciding to what degree reason and sentiment
enter into moral decisions. He emphasizes once again the importance
of determining matters of fact, but he insists that the final factor in
determining moral decisions is the factor of sentiment. An action is
virtuous, if, upon being considered by reference to factual matters, a
feeling of approbation arises with regard to the action.

Ultimate ends as determined by sentiment

According to Hume, then, the "ultimate ends" of human action
are determined not by reason, but by what he calls "sentiment." It
makes sense to ask a man why he wants money; his answer is that it
is an "instrument of pleasure." But it makes no sense to ask *why* he
wants pleasure: "Something must be desirable on its own account,
and because of its immediate accord or agreement with human sentiment and affection."

Hume rejects the claim that all actions are motivated by self-love.

The "social virtues of humanity and benevolence" are as natural as the tendency to seek benefits for oneself. Even justice, which is based on social utility, is a "natural" virtue in the sense that it is related to reason and the sentiments, which are natural. "If self-love, if benevolence be natural to man," he writes, "if reason and forethought be also natural; then may the same epithet be applied to justice, order, fidelity, property, society."

VII

KANT: DUTY AS
ACTION THAT CAN
BE UNIVERSALIZED

Immanuel Kant (1724–1804), whose concern for men as ends (not as mere instruments to be used for the satisfaction of others) reflects his Pietistic background, is noteworthy as a philosopher who attempted, by the use of reason, to construct foundations for morality. The effort to show by rational means alone the necessity for acting in accordance with moral principles that govern all men was made with great seriousness and incisiveness by this Germanic thinker. Although those who regard the foundations of morality to be provided by the nonrational promptings of passionately directed men may regard as paradoxical or even absurd the attempt to legislate conduct by rational considerations alone, anyone interested in ethics is forced to admit that Kant's contributions must be respected and, if possible, accomodated to any satisfactory theory of morality.

Kant's most important ethical work is his *Foundations of the Metaphysics of Morals*, published in 1785. The author explains in the preface to this work that the book was written as a preliminary to a metaphysics of morals. To explain here the relations of what Kant calls the "pure practical reason" to the "pure speculative reason," already discussed with great creativity and subtlety in Kant's

Critique of Pure Reason (1781), would be to undertake a task that would move the author beyond the problem that is most useful and least confusing to the general reader— namely, the problem of setting forth and clarifying "the supreme principle of morality." Kant explains that his treatise proceeds from an understanding of "the common rational knowledge of morals"—the moral principles everyone who thinks clearly can recognize—to the philosophical knowledge of morals, and then on to the foundations of a metaphysics of morals and a critical examination of pure practical reason. Although these terms are not initially meaningful to the reader unacquainted with Kant's previous work, the direction of the book is clear; the essay moves from moral beliefs to the highly theoretical rational foundations of those beliefs.

The good will as good in itself

"Nothing in the world—indeed nothing even beyond the world—can possibly be conceived which could be called good without qualification except a *good will*," declares Kant in the opening sentence of the First Section of the *Foundations*. The philosopher quickly rejects, as good in themselves, various virtues and "gifts of fortune" which other philosophers have prized as good on their own account, whatever the circumstances: intelligence, wit, judgment, courage, resoluteness, perseverance, power, riches, honor, health, happiness, and prosperity of any sort. None of these features of character or states of being can justifiably be said to be "good without qualification," Kant insists. Virtues of mind and character can easily be misused if the will that directs them is not a good will, while the states of good fortune which men value—the enjoyment of wealth, honor, or power—can foster pride and arrogance, unless the actions of fortunate men are controlled by a good will.

Kant concedes the moral utility of the classical virtues of moderation, self-control, and calm deliberation, but he argues that such moral qualities, which contribute to the moral value of action, are dependent upon the good will for their direction and hence are not worthwhile on their own account.

The question as to what something which is good is good *for* makes sense only when asked of that which derives its value from its use. Consequently, Kant does not attempt to show what the good will is good *for*; he argues, on the contrary, that the good will is good not because of what it achieves but simply "because of its willing, i.e., it is good of itself."

Even if the will were to prove ineffectual in accomplishing its purpose, a good will—by which, as Kant is careful to point out, is meant "not . . . a mere wish but . . . the summoning of all the means in our power"—is so much worthwhile for its own sake that "it would sparkle like a jewel in its own right, as something that had its full worth in itself."

Kant argues that if the happiness of man—man possessed of reason and will—were the end of nature, instinct, not reason, would be given the guidance of the will. The fact that reason cannot competently guide the will with regard to the satisfaction of human needs indicates that reason's function must be, not to provide for the realization of happiness, but to produce a will good in itself. The goal of nature appears to be the realization of purposes prescribed by reason on formal grounds, without regard for the ends determined by the inclinations or desires of men.

The good will, although it is good in itself, is not the only good, Kant concedes, but it is "the highest good and the condition of all others, even of the desire for happiness."

Moral worth as dependent upon the good will

An act has moral worth only if it is done from duty, Kant next maintains. The good will is good in itself, and its value is such that if an act is determined by such a will, the act has moral worth. But if the determination is from practical considerations or as a result of natural inclinations, the resultant act, whether or not it be in accord with duty, has no moral worth.

The proposition that moral worth depends on the determining power of the good will is illustrated by the following examples. If a dealer does not overcharge an inexperienced customer, his act is in accordance with duty. But such an act is to the merchant's advantage, for if he overcharges his customers, his business suffers. If, then, he desists from overcharging because to do so helps his business, his act has no moral worth. Only if he withstood the temptation to overcharge because to charge more than the merchandise is worth would be contrary to the requirements of a good will would his act have moral worth.

Preserving one's life because one has an inclination to do so, or being kind because one is sympathetically drawn to others, or securing one's own happiness—all these are modes of behavior in accordance with duty (to act otherwise would be to act wrongly). But such conduct has moral worth only if it is prompted by the will, only if one persists in such conduct despite any inclination to do otherwise, and despite any practical disadvantage in so acting.

Moral worth as a matter of principle

Having presumably established the points that only a good will is good in itself, and that an action has moral worth only if it is done from duty as prescribed by a good will, Kant sets forth the next basic proposition of morality: "An action performed from duty does not have its moral worth in the purpose which is to be achieved through it but in the maxim by which it is determined." That is, for Kant, an action has moral worth because of the principle involved, not because of the value of the consequences. What actually results from an action is not *morally* significant; the whole moral value of an action lies in the formal character of the principle which determines it. (Kant later indicates the features which provide a maxim with its value as a formal prescription.)

Kant then explains that the formal character of a moral principle has value because it provides the principle with what is necessary to its status as a moral law. Duty itself is defined as "the necessity of an action executed from respect for law." When the will is itself determined by nothing but the moral law, it is a good will; and when an act is determined by nothing but respect for duty, it is therefore determined by respect for the moral law. Again, Kant stresses the point that it is not the result of what is done that affects the moral worth of an action; the whole value of an action is dependent upon respect for and deliberate obedience to the moral law.

The categorical imperative

The moral law, which only a rational being could conceive, must be of a formal sort. If the results of an action do not determine the moral worth of the action, then it must be the *form* of the action, as set forth in the moral law, that wins the respect and assent of the good will. Kant concludes that the fundamental moral principle that binds the will is such as to suggest the following injunction: "I should never act in such a way that I could not also will that my maxim should be a universal law." If the principle governing the will is rational, it is formal; if it is formal, it is universal. The conclusion, then, is that an act has moral worth if it is done from the conviction that the principle of the action is capable of being universalized—that is, made applicable to all persons.

Kant distinguishes between two kinds of "imperatives," or commands governing the action of the will: *hypothetical* imperatives and *categorical* imperatives. An action is hypothetically imperative if it is necessary to the attainment of something *desired*: You *must* do such-and-such, *if* you want a certain result.

A categorical imperative, on the other hand, applies no matter what one desires. The moral necessity to act is unconditional. Kant declares, "The categorical imperative would be one which presented an action as of itself objectively necessary, without regard to any other end." That is, an act is categorically obligatory if the maxim of the act is one of which reason would approve—if the kind of act required is one capable of being universalized. A statement of the sort, "You ought to do such-and-such; there are no ifs, ands, or buts about it," reflects the categorical character of the moral imperative.

According to Kant, the categorical imperative is an *a priori* synthetic proposition. The necessity of the will's acting in accordance with the law of reason is *a priori*, in that the necessity is in no way dependent upon circumstances or factual considerations. But the connection is synthetic in that it is not logically analytic: one cannot deduce the necessity of the will's action from any other matter—either from the operations of reason or from the inclinations of any person.

Four examples

To illustrate how one could decide a question of duty through the use of the categorical imperative, Kant offers four examples.

He first of all considers the question of suicide for one "reduced to despair by a series of evils . . . ." The question to be asked is whether the maxim of the action could become a universal law of nature. Kant declares that the maxim of the action is: "For love of myself, I make it my principle to shorten my life when by a longer duration it threatens more evil that satisfaction." But such a maxim could not become a universal law of nature, Kant concludes, for it would be contradictory "to destroy life by the feeling whose special office is to impel the improvement of life."

Kant next considers the moral problem of a person who needs to borrow money but knows he cannot repay it. The man considers promising to repay the loan, even though he knows that he cannot keep his promise. The maxim of the action, according to Kant, is: "When I believe myself to be in need of money, I will borrow money and promise to repay it, although I know I shall never do so." But such a maxim, converted into a universal law, becomes self-defeating (contradicts itself), in that no one would lend money if the principle of useless promises became universal.

Could indulgence in pleasure and the neglect of one's talents possibly be one's duty? The maxim to neglect the development of one's creative faculties and to give oneself to a life of idle amusement could not be willed to become a universal law of nature, Kant claims, for such a person, "as a rational being . . . necessarily wills that all his faculties should be developed." (The conception of a rational but self-indulgent man is self-contradictory.)

Finally, Kant considers a man who, enjoying good fortune, is tempted to ignore the hardships of others and to contribute nothing to their welfare. Such a maxim, if universalized, would be self-defeating in that the man would himself have ruled out the possibility of receiving assistance from others whenever, by a change of fortune, he needed their aid.

The impossibility of willing the universalization of a maxim may either be internal—whenever the conception of such a universal law is logically inconsistent—or self-defeating. Duty holds for all rational beings, Kant insists, and hence the law of moral action is objective. There is never any use in considering whether it is to one's advantage to act in a certain way or whether one is inclined to do so. If one is to act dutifully one must do so as prompted by the consideration that the maxim of the act is such that one could will it to become a universal law of nature.

Men are often inclined to take into account contingent circumstances—the factual matters that make a difference to the utility of what is done. But to give priority to the empirical is to neglect the law of reason, which puts complete stress on the formal and universal. In fact, Kant emphasizes, morality has nothing whatsover to do with considerations provided by experience. Kant departs from his ordinarily dispassionate style in order to underscore the warning against mixing morality with the empirical:

Thus everything empirical is not only wholly unworthy to be an ingredient in the principle of morality but is even highly prejudicial to the purity of moral practices themselves. . . . We cannot too much or too often warn against the lax or even base manner of thought which seeks principles among empirical motives and laws, for human reason in its weariness is glad to rest on this pillow. In a dream of sweet illusions (in which it embraces not Juno but a cloud), it substi-

tutes for morality a bastard patched up from limbs of very different
parentage, which looks like anything one wishes to see in it, but not
like virtue to anyone who has ever beheld her in her true form.

Perhaps no other passage in Kant better emphasizes the author's
insistence upon confining morality to an area of concern defined by
reason alone. The appeal to formal considerations in the judgment of
persons and actions is here passionately made in such a manner as to
suggest that although Kant presumed his foundations of the metaphysics of morals to be demanded by the nature of morality, his
entire range of inquiry was controlled by an unyielding preconcep-
tion of the matters that might properly be described as "moral."

Kant introduces metaphysical considerations into his discussion
of ethics, but he contends that the metaphysics of morals must be
distinguished from speculative metaphysics. A metaphysics of morals
calls for "objectively practical laws," which Kant defines as distinct
from empirical laws and as determined only by reason. A study of
the relation of inclinations to actions belongs to empirical psychology, he argues, but a study of how the will would operate were
it determined by reason alone belongs to the metaphysics of morals.
To understand what *ought* to happen involves understanding what
would happen, *if* the will were acting in a wholly rational manner;
that is, on the basis of objective—universally valid, *a priori*—
principles.

Men as ends in themselves

Ends of action are "material," according to Kant, when they are
ends only relative to persons (subjects); such ends are subjective. An
objective end, therefore, is of absolute, not relative, worth; and it
must be an end in itself—not something related as a means to something else, and not something dependent for its value on someone's
inclination to secure it.

Kant's decision is that "rational nature exists as an end in itself,"
and hence that man is an end in himself and is not merely a means.
The distinction between "things" and "persons" is precisely the distinction between that which has only relative worth, as a means, and
that the existence of which is an end in itself.

The categorical imperative, originally stated as, "Act only according to that maxim by which you can at the same time will that it
should become a universal law," may now be recast as a practical

imperative: "Act so that you treat humanity, whether in your own person or in that of another, always as an end and never as a means only."

The four examples of moral problems, previously considered by reference to the categorical imperative, are reconsidered, but now by reference to the practical imperative.

A man cannot commit suicide and have done his duty, for such action is directly opposed to the principle of treating one's own person as an end; by destroying himself, he uses himself as a means to the end of his depression.

If a promise is made without the intention to keep the promise, the act is contrary to duty, for the person deceived is then used as a means to the resolution of a practical problem.

A person who neglects the development of his talents fails to treat himself as an end, for although he does not destroy himself as an end, he fails to realize the full value of himself as an end; consequently, he mistreats himself considered as an end.

Finally, a person who neglects his duty to others, in that he neglects persons who are ends in themselves, fails to act in accordance with the practical imperative. Everyone must work to further the ends of others, Kant insists, for "the ends of any person, who is an end in himself, must as far as possible also be my end, if that conception of an end in itself is to have its full effect on me."

Man as legislator in the realm of ends

A third form of the moral imperative is based on the claim that a rational will can have as its object only itself as generating universal laws. Rational beings, as bound by universal laws given by the rational will, form what Kant calls "a realm of ends." A human being is, then, a legislator in the realm of ends; as such, a person has a "dignity" or intrinsic worth that is not to be compared with the "market price" of ends related to human inclinations. The third formula may be stated as follows: So act that "the will through its maxims could regard itself at the same time as universally lawgiving." For the will to regard itself as universally lawgiving is for the will to place itself and every other person under the law of reason. Hence, the moral principle requires that every act of will be sanctioned by a law that the will itself legislates.

The property of the will by which it is a law to itself Kant calls "the autonomy of the will." He regards such autonomy as central to all morality. The will is free in that in legislating universally, it rules for itself; "... a free will and a will under moral laws are identical."

Kant asks why it is that a rational being should subject itself to the universal law that the free will gives. "I will admit," he answers, "that no interest impels me to do so .... But I must nevertheless take an interest in it and see how it comes about, for this 'ought' is properly a 'would' that is valid for every rational being provided reason is practical for him without hindrance." What a person *would* do were his will directed by reason (and, hence, by a universal law legislated by the will), is what the person, as a moral subject, *ought* to do.

To think of ourselves as "free," Kant declares, is to "transport ourselves into the intelligible world as members of it and know the autonomy of the will together with its consequence, morality ...." To think of ourselves as "obligated," on the other hand, is to "consider ourselves as belonging both to the world of sense and at the same time to the intelligible world." Man is bound by the laws of nature insofar as he belongs to "the world of sense," but he is free insofar as his will is morally autonomous.

Kant concedes that it is not possible to explain how man considered as intelligence, as a thing-in-itself in the intelligible world, can provide a moral incentive for action. The problem of explaining how pure reason can be practical is insoluble. But morality presupposes the autonomy of the will and its power to legislate universally and to move itself in accordance with the laws it generates. The idea of the intelligible world is more negative than positive: "This intelligible world signifies only a something which remains when I have excluded from the determining ground of my will everything belonging to the world of sense in order to withhold the principle of motives from the field of sensibility." But it is important that one respect a person whose will is a good will. Such a person belongs to the "universal realm of ends-in-themselves," and we can belong to that realm "only when we carefully conduct ourselves according to maxims of freedom as if they were laws of nature."

Throughout Kant's *Metaphysics of Morals* the emphasis is upon reason as providing the moral law. Since reason is concerned purely with form, the moral law is formal; and since no formal law makes any reference to conditions that may change, the moral law is universal. The assertion of the intrinsic worth of the good will, and of persons as rational beings, is based upon the belief that if human beings, as moral beings, cannot derive moral worth from the consequences of their actions—since consequences are contingent upon circumstances—then the value of persons must reside in the autonomy of the will as obedient to its own laws, which are laws of reason.

There is in Kant's ethics, then, nothing of the emphasis upon useful action, socially beneficial conduct, or human happiness that has marked the work of such classical moral philosophers as the skeptics and Epicureans, and such modern ones as the utilitarians and pragmatists, for whom action and the results of action are central in morality. Kant's "practical reason" is pure reason put to work; it is not pure reason as attracted by possibilities within the world of sense.

Consequently, it is not surprising that Kant has harsh words for those who would lead morality away from universal formal considerations and into the world of appetites and demanding inclinations. Kant's warning is clear: "If the will seeks the law which is to determine it anywhere else than in the fitness of its maxims to its own universal legislation, and if it thus goes outside itself and seeks this law in the property of any of its subjects, heteronomy always results." Autonomy, or self-government through the use of reason, is the will's proper business in the moral sphere; heteronomy, or government by something outside the will, is the fate of a will that has lost its freedom by giving itself over to objects.

Of all the objects that might intrude upon the will and, by seducing it, destroy its power to rule itself, the most objectionable is one's own happiness. Kant declares that the principle of one's own happiness is morally corrupting because it "supports morality with incentives that undermine it and destroy all its sublimity, for it puts the motives to virtue and those to vice in the same class . . . ."

The attempt to base morality on the search for perfection is useless, Kant claims, because one must presuppose morality in order to build the conception of perfection. And to attempt to build morality upon the idea of a perfect divine will—the theological way—is even worse. This approach is untenable in that not only must the idea of the divine also be based on moral conceptions—and hence be circular—but, furthermore, one is tempted to take as ideals the destructive features of "glory and dominion combined with the awful conceptions of might and vengeance . . . ."

Imperatives related to objects—such as happiness and perfection—are conditional imperatives; consequently, Kant argues, such imperatives cannot be moral, for moral imperatives are categorical. The rejection of any ethics based upon empirical principles follows from this basic consideration. Morality demands a good will, and the good will is autonomous, rationally directed, and legislative in the realm of ends; as such, the will is good in itself, without qualification. This proposition constitutes the foundation of Kant's metaphysics of morals.

VIII

⋐⋍⋙⋰⋙⋰⋙⋰⋙⋱

MILL: RIGHT
ACTS AS PRODUCTIVE
OF HAPPINESS

The Scottish philosopher John Stuart Mill (1806-1873) represents the survival in modern philosophy of the Epicurean idea that happiness is the good, and that actions are right to the degree that they are productive of happiness and wrong insofar as they are not. Mill's ethics bears many points of resemblance to the ethical views of his predecessor Jeremy Bentham (1748-1832), who also declared happiness to be the end of conduct, but Mill did not agree with Bentham's claim that every man must, as a law of nature, seek his own pleasure, nor did Mill believe that pleasures vary only in quantity (intensity and duration). In opposition to Bentham's exclusive concern with quantity, Mill insisted that pleasures vary also in *quality* and that, consequently, anyone, in deciding what to do, ought to take into account not only the amount of pleasure (or happiness) to be gained by his action (for himself and others), but also the *kinds* of pleasures involved.

Since Mill's emphasis in ethics is upon the utility of actions—that is, upon their usefulness in the production of happiness—he chose the name "Utilitarianism" to designate the kind of view he held, and thereby he placed himself in clear opposition to any kind of *formal-*

ism. Unlike Kant, then, who regarded the form or principle of an action as the source of its moral worth (since principles, as purely formal, appeal to reason quite apart from any considerations of interest or inclination), Mill confidently declared that morality is on the right track only when it aims at happiness or pleasure. Thus, Mill made the desires of men (and not their reason) the final determinants of value in morality as well as in matters of appetite.

Mill states clearly that the basic proposition advanced in his *Utilitarianism* (1863) is "that actions are right in proportion as they tend to promote happiness, wrong as they tend to produce the reverse of happiness." No effort is made to discourage the identification of happiness and pleasure: "By happiness is intended pleasure, and the absence of pain; by unhappiness, pain, and the privation of pleasure."

Pleasure as good in itself

In distinctive contrast to Kant, who regarded the good will as the only thing good in itself, Mill unabashedly identifies pleasure as the intrinsically good end of action: "pleasure, and freedom from pain, are the only things desirable as ends; . . . all desirable things (which are as numerous in the utilitarian as in any other scheme) are desirable either for the pleasure inherent in themselves, or as a means to the promotion of pleasure and the prevention of pain."

The Utilitarians had difficulty with the critics. Mill reports that the emphasis upon the utility of actions led some philosophical critics to charge the Utilitarians with neglecting aesthetic pleasures and the joys of mere amusement (a neglect which would clearly be uncharacteristic of enthusiastic hedonists like Mill), while the concentration upon pleasure as the focal point of all moral concern prompted "the very same persons" to charge Utilitarianism with being "too practicably voluptuous . . . ." Mill comments on the fact that the kind of theory he defends tends to provoke "inveterate dislike" in many opponents; and he sardonically sums up the uncompromising critical attitude of those who reject Utilitarianism: "To suppose that life has (as they express it) no higher end than pleasure—no better and nobler object of desire and pursuit—they designate as utterly mean and grovelling, as a doctrine worthy only of swine, to whom the followers of Epicurus were, at a very early period, contemptuously likened; and modern holders of the doctrine are occasionally made the subject of equally polite comparison by its German, French, and English assailants."

In opposition to the criticism that Utilitarianism is "a doctrine worthy only of swine," Mill replies that it is the critics of Utilitarianism, not the Utilitarians, who have such a low view of man as to suppose him capable of no pleasure of which swine are not capable. He concedes that Utilitarian writers generally have placed mental pleasures above bodily ones because of the "circumstantial advantages" of the former—their "greater permanency, safety, uncostliness," and other quantitative features. But Mill then adds, in a statement that has become famous and by which his view is marked off from those of other hedonists, "It is quite compatible with the principle of utility to recognize the fact that some kinds of pleasure are more desirable and more valuable than others." It is in this insistence that pleasures vary in kind, or quality—as well as in quantity—that Mill's ethical theory achieves its unique and provocative aspect.

The test of qualitative difference

A difference in the quality of pleasure is determined, Mill claims, by the preference of those who distinguish among pleasures irrespective of their quantity. If one pleasure is preferred to another, even though the two are quantitatively alike—for example, are of the same intensity and duration—it must be that the pleasures vary qualitatively, or in kind; it is then the difference of feeling, not of amount, that accounts for the preference. (Even though Mill does not develop the implications of this pragmatic test, it is evident that pleasures could vary qualitatively even though they were equally desirable. A person might be the kind of person who finds equally desirable the pleasant experience of being at the seashore and the pleasant experience of being in the mountains, and he might find that he does not prefer the one kind of experience to the other except when there are quantitative differences—that is, when one of the experiences contains *more* pleasure than the other.)

A clear-cut case of qualitative difference, Mill suggests, can be found wherever a clear majority of those acquainted with two kinds of pleasures tend to prefer the one kind to the other, even when the quantity is equal. "Of two pleasures," he writes, "if there be one to which all or almost all who have experience of both give a decided preference, irrespective of any feeling of moral obligation to prefer it, that is the more desirable pleasure." (Mill later defends his use of the term "desirable" as a synonym for "valuable.") The expression "superiority in quality" is explained in the following careful statement:

> If one of the two pleasures is, by those who are competently acquainted with both, placed so far above the other that they prefer it, even though knowing it to be attended with a greater amount of discontent, and would not resign it for any quantity of the other pleasure which their nature is capable of, we are justified in ascribing to the preferred enjoyment a superiority in quality, so far outweighing quantity as to render it, in comparison, of small account.

Lower and higher pleasures

Mill next contends that those who are acquainted with both the "lower" and the "higher" pleasures—those of the beast and those of the human being who exercises his intelligence and maintains his sense of dignity—"do give a most marked preference to the manner of existence which employs their higher faculties." No one who has enjoyed the use of the higher faculties, Mill argues, would ever trade his happiness for the pleasures of a beast, no matter how intense a beast's pleasures might be. Of course, Mill concedes, the human being recognizes that his happiness is far from perfect, and he may become dissatisfied because of the limitations on the exercise of his human faculties, but, Mill declares firmly, "It is better to be a human being dissatisfied than a pig satisfied; better to be Socrates dissatisfied than a fool satisfied."

Those who are acquainted with both the higher and the lower pleasures—with the pleasures of the intellect, feelings, and imagination, as well as with the pleasures of "mere sensation"—are in a better position to judge the values of pleasures according to quality than are those who, like the pig and the fool, know only the pleasures of sensation. Mill acknowledges the fact that men often choose the "lower" pleasures instead of the "higher," but he attributes the preference for what is known to be of lesser qualitative value to "temptation," "infirmity of character," and the subsequent loss of the capacity for "the nobler feelings."

The proof of desirability

In a later chapter concerning the sort of proof that can be advanced in support of the principle of utility, Mill returns to the analysis of the conditions under which a judgment of value can be established. He contends that "Questions about ends are, in other words, questions what things are desirable." The problem, then, becomes that of deciding how one determines that happiness is desirable. Even more fundamental is the question as to how one determines, with reference to whatever is said to be desirable as an end, that it is indeed desirable. In a famous argument, which has become a target for critics, Mill draws an analogy by which he attempts to show how proof of desirability is possible:

The only proof capable of being given that an object is visible is that people actually see it. The only proof that a sound is audible is that people hear it; and so of the other sources of our experience. In like manner, I apprehend, the sole evidence it is possible to produce that anything is desirable is that people do actually desire it. If the end which the utilitarian doctrine proposes to itself were not, in theory and in practice, acknowledged to be an end, nothing could ever convince any person that it was so. No reason can be given why the general happiness is desirable, except that each person, so far as he believes it to be attainable, desires his own happiness. This, however, being a fact, we have not only all the proof which the case admits of, but all which it is possible to require, that happiness is a good, that each person's happiness is a good to that person, and the general happiness, therefore, a good to the aggregate of all persons. . . .

In contending that happiness is desirable because it is desired, Mill presumes that the desire is indicative of value because it is aroused by happiness itself. A thing is desired because a person finds, through experience, that he cares for it, not merely as a means, but for its own sake.

There is no reason to suppose that Mill committed the kind of mistake he is often charged with—that of proposing that any object whatsoever is to be regarded as "desirable" or worthwhile provided simply that it is desired, even though one may be in ignorance of its true character. The qualifications involved in Mill's account of the test of qualitative value differences make the circumstance that a person be "completely acquainted" with an object of desire *a condition of proving* that the desired object is, in virtue of being desired, desirable.

Although Mill attempted to establish "the general happiness" as an end of action, by arguing that since each person's happiness is a good to that person, the general happiness is "a good to the aggregate of all persons," many critics have pointed out that there is no such collective entity as the "aggregate of all persons" which can be considered to be something over and above the collection of individual persons with their individual preferences. Even though each person may desire his own happiness, there is no resultant tendency for any one person to desire the happiness of all.

Consideration of objections

Mill considers various objections to the Utilitarian claim that since happiness is the end of human action, the basic principle of morality must be that an action is right insofar as it tends to promote human happiness. He first of all considers the objection that happiness is unattainable and that, in any case, men can do without happiness and, in fact, have no right to it.

In response to such an objection, Mill argues that the Utilitarians have never suggested that life ought to be, or could be, a life of constant rapture or "highly pleasurable excitement." A life of moderate pleasures and few pains is surely possible and thus can serve as an objective of human action. Human beings generally are capable of enjoying the pleasures of the intellect and of the faculties of appreciation, and anyone can profit from a certain amount of "mental culture." Nor is there any reason why a person cannot find that his happiness does not depend solely upon the satisfaction of his own individual needs and desires: "Genuine private affections and a sincere interest in the public good are possible, though in unequal degrees, to every rightly brought up human being."

Mill agrees that men can do without happiness, and he points out that living without happiness "is done involuntarily by nineteen-twentieths of mankind." But he insists that even the moral hero who sacrifices his happiness for others does so not because virtue is an end in itself, but in order that those he serves be relieved of suffering or provided with a happiness that would otherwise be denied them.

Some critics have accused the Utilitarians of fostering an egoistic morality, a morality that places the highest moral value on the search for one's own pleasure. But Mill contends that Utilitarianism requires that each person be "as strictly impartial as a disinterested and benevolent spectator" in considering choices between his own happiness and that of another. Mill urges that education be directed toward fostering an habitual association between each man's personal happiness and the general happiness of those his action affects.

Ironically, although Utilitarianism has by some critics been charged with being a selfish ethical system, others have contended that the Utilitarian doctrine requires more of men than they can reasonably be expected to provide. To ask a man to forsake his own happiness for that of others is to put an unreasonable demand upon human nature. Mill's response to this objection is that Utilitarianism does not require that every moral action be motivated by a concern for the happiness of others. The doctrine merely specifies what it is that makes an action morally right—namely, its tendency to add to the sum of human happiness. In clear opposition to the Kantian idea that the moral worth of an action depends upon its having been done out of respect for the moral law, Mill maintains that the "multiplication of happiness" is the moral objective—if the "public utility" is served, it makes no moral difference whether the act by which the general happiness is achieved is motivated by considerations of "private utility" or not.

Another objection made to Utilitarianism is that the emphasis upon the consequences of actions tends to encourage the Utilitarian to neglect the moral worth of human beings. In the concern for the utility of actions, the Utilitarian fails to be sympathetic toward those whose character and motives are worthwhile.

Mill agrees that the Utilitarian emphasis is upon the utility of acts, but he denies that such an emphasis involves being blind to the moral worth of persons. He does affirm, however, that if a trait of character, presumably virtuous, were to lead to actions that did more harm than good, bringing about unhappiness and making happiness impossible, the Utilitarian would be inclined to regard such a character trait as morally bad and the actions resulting from it as morally wrong. As for the tendency of some Utilitarians to confuse the moral value of actions with the moral worth of persons, or to regard the two as entirely independent, Mill claims that the Utilitarian is no more liable to such errors than is the proponent of any other ethical theory.

Mill considers also the objections that Utilitarianism is a godless doctrine, that it is an endorsement of expediency over principle, and

that it is impractical in that it calls for more calculation of consequences than a moral agent is able to manage. In reply, Mill maintains that it is reasonable to suppose that God wills the happiness of
His creatures, and he suggests that the Utilitarian has as much right
as any other to regard religion as a source of illumination in the
moral sphere. In answer to the charge of expediency, Mill points out
that Utilitarianism emphasizes what is useful for all concerned; it
does not sanction self-centered conduct. Nor does the Utilitarian
approve of the specious reasoning which leads a person, for the sake
of an immediate gain, to violate rules whose general utility has been
well established. Finally, as to the difficulty of calculation, Mill
comments that all responsible moral deliberation involves making
use of habits of action and general procedures already supported by
reference to the principle underlying moral judgment. The Christian
is not expected to read through the Old and New Testaments before
acting; analogously, the Utilitarian is not compelled to calculate, in
great detail, the consequences in terms of happiness and unhappiness
of a proposed course of conduct.

Moral sanctions

A very important question in ethics, as Mill claims, is the question
of an ultimate sanction of a moral standard. The philosopher who
presumes to set forth a method for determining whether acts are
morally right or wrong must be prepared to defend his proposal by
making clear the source of the obligation to act in accordance with
the basic principle involved.

For the principle of utility, according to Mill, there are both
external and internal sanctions. The external sanctions are provided
by the approval of both men and God; men generally approve action
that aims at their happiness, and God is ordinarily conceived to be a
spirit whose concern is for the general happiness. The internal sanction of the Utilitarian standard is, like any moral sanction, "a subjective feeling in our own minds"—a disinterested feeling, connected
with the idea of duty, which becomes a pain "more or less intense,"
whenever duty is violated. The faculty called "Conscience," Mill
writes, is the source of this disinterested feeling by which a principle
of morality is finally approved or rejected. There is what Mill calls "a
natural basis of sentiment" in support of the Utilitarian method of
resolving moral problems; society is a powerful force in the influence

of conscience, and as a result of the unifying power of social sentiment, men come to feel that action is morally right if, without
granting special privileges to anyone, it aims at the happiness of the
group.

A distinction is made between *desire* and *will* in Mill's ethics. The
"power of habit" makes it possible for the will to overcome desires
that might lead to self-defeating or socially injurious action. A person not initially inclined to choose the virtuous course of action can
be motivated to do so if he comes to associate doing the right thing
with pleasure. "How can the will to be virtuous, where it does not
exist in sufficient force, be implanted or awakened?" Mill asks; and
he answers, "Only by making the person desire virtue—by making
him think of it in a pleasurable light, or of its absence in a painful
one."

Justice and utility

Mill recognizes the force of the traditional idea that justice and
utility, or the just and the expedient, are opposed. He comments on
the tendency of persons to suppose that justice is somehow absolute
and that it is a conception that has its origin in nature.

In order to make the connection between justice and utility clear,
Mill examines the question as to whether the feeling of justice is
fundamental and distinctive, *sui generis*, or a "derivative feeling,
formed by a combination of others." He first of all asks whether
there is some quality common to all actions that would be regarded
as unjust—thereby hoping to isolate an opposing feature that would
characterize just acts.

Upon examination of acts that would be considered unjust, however, Mill finds no one common feature. Acts are regarded as unjust
if they violate someone's legal rights (although there are exceptions),
or if they deprive someone of something to which he has a moral
right, or if they deny to someone what he deserves, or grant to him
what he does not deserve. It is unjust to break faith or to be
partial—to deny the principle of equality. There appears to be no
"mental link," Mill points out, by which these various kinds of acts
can be regarded as exhibiting a common feature.

Mill next examines the etymology of the word "just," and finds
that the word, literally, means "conformity to law." However, the
recognition of men's fallibility has led to a use of the term "just"

such that an act is just if and only if it is in accordance with "laws as ought to exist, including such as ought to exist but do not . . . ." The conception of justice, then, is very close to that of moral obligation.

Duty appears to be opposed to prudence, Mill suggests, because duty is "exacted," while it would not ordinarily make sense to speak of "exacting" from a person what it would be only prudent for him to do. Morality can be distinguished from "simple expediency" by the feature of *punishment*: "We do not call anything wrong, unless we mean to imply that a person ought to be punished in some way or other for doing it; if not by law, by the opinion of his fellow creatures; if not by opinion, by the reproaches of his own conscience."

Justice may be distinguished from beneficence by the presence, in any case of justice, of a right that has to be recognized and served. A generous person may be right in helping another, even though the other has no right to be helped; but if an act is just, it would be wrong not to do it, for there is a right that would be neglected were the act not done.

Justice is not to be identified with the morally right, then, in that there are moral obligations that do not arise from the rights of others.

Returning to the question as to the origin of the sentiment of justice, Mill concludes that although the feeling of justice does not arise from considerations of expediency since it consists of the desire to punish a person who has done harm, it is nevertheless true that expediency is fundamental to morality. Mill suggests that Kant's moral imperative, "So act that thy rule of conduct might be adopted as a law by all rational beings," be modified to read "we ought to shape our conduct by a rule which all rational beings might adopt with benefit to their collective interest." The "sentiment of justice," then, is not itself moral, but the implicit reference to the general good is a moral reference.

Mill offers a clarification of the meaning of the expression "a right." He contends that when we say that something is a person's "right," "we mean that he has a valid claim on society to protect him in the possession of it, either by the force of law, or by that of education and opinion." A right is whatever society is obligated to secure for an individual; any benefit that a man seeks which is not a benefit that society must secure for him is not a moral right. The basis of society's obligation, Mill argues, is the general utility of the act of securing the right for the individual. The intensity of the sentiment for retaliation when a right is violated cannot be accounted for by the recognition of this utility, however; there is "an animal element" in the sentiment of justice which responds to any threat to the security of the individual. The moral "ought" becomes the forceful "must" because of the animal insistence upon conduct insuring the rights and security of the individual.

Differences of opinion concerning the justice or injustice of punishment will persist, according to Mill, just so long as considerations of utility are separated from considerations of justice. Mill rejects the idea of an absolutely isolated "free will," by which men presumably escape the determining effects of their environments, thereby making themselves liable to moral judgment. He also dismisses the conception of a social contract, by which men presumably, at some far distant time in the past, agreed to abide by certain laws for the good of all. And, finally, he sets aside, as representing a primitive conception of justice, the idea that the punishment must fit the crime, "the *lex talionis*, an eye for an eye, and a tooth for a tooth."

The attempt to solve moral problems by reference to any standard other than that of social utility leads to unanswerable dilemmas, Mill argues. On the one hand, it seems fair and proper to reward the more productive or more skilled worker with larger wages than those given to workers who, although doing the best they can, do not measure up to the superior man. On the other hand, if the worker whose skill is not so marked is not compensated for his effort and for being denied the adulation given the superior worker, justice appears to be denied. Only a consideration of social utility settles the matter (and does so, of course, in favor of the superior worker).

Again, problems of taxation can be debated endlessly, depending on the inclinations and philosophical perspectives of the parties to the debate. If all benefit equally, all should pay equally—so runs one argument. If some have greater wealth than others, they should pay more of the costs of government—so runs the counter claim. Only Utilitarian principles offer a way of resolving such an issue, Mill insists.

Of the moral rules by which the relationships among men are ordered, none are more important, Mill contends, than those by which men are restrained from harming one another. Mill recognizes the utility of practical principles that set forth the most efficient ways of managing certain affairs—such principles are of positive benefit generally—but unless men of power are kept from exercising their power at the expense of others, injustice results. In short, the rules that protect men are of greater importance than are those rules which aim at providing benefits.

Mill's conclusion concerning the relationship of justice to expediency is that justice, in attempting to insure that men do not injure others or deprive them of goods, and in endorsing retributive action when harm is done, is superior to a "simple" expediency. But the defense of the traditional maxims of justice is finally seen to be Utilitarian. "It appears . . . that justice is a name for certain moral requirements, which, regarded collectively, stand higher in the scale of social utility, and are therefore of more paramount obligation, than any others . . . ."

The principles of justice, then, turn out to be general principles of action based upon Utilitarian considerations. Exceptions to general maxims are called for, consequently, whenever the usual advantage of a mode of action is offset by the features of a particular case. "Thus, to save a life," Mill writes, "it may not only be allowable, but a duty, to steal, or take by force, the necessary food or medicine, or to kidnap, and compel to officiate, the only qualified medical practitioner."

Mill's original claims remain after his exhaustive analysis of the relation of justice to Utilitarian considerations. An act is right to the degree that it promotes happiness and diminishes unhappiness. Some pleasures are better than others because of qualitative differences. Everything considered, the "higher" pleasures of the intellect, imagination, and moral sentiments are superior to the bodily pleasures, and the social good takes priority over the good of the individual. When apparent conflicts between considerations of justice and utility develop, a resolution in favor of social utility is morally preferable.

IX

MOORE: GOODNESS
AS UNANALYZABLE

Although the question of the *summum bonum*—the highest good—has preoccupied philosophers for centuries, another problem, central to ethics, has also intrigued those who would clarify and appraise the judgments of morality—the problem of *goodness*. Plato thought that the good—not *what* is good, but goodness itself—is an Idea, a universal Form, in which anything that is good "participates." Aristotle regarded the good as "that at which all things aim"; for him, the property goodness was understandable only by reference to "ends" as related to the essential functions of things. Epicurus, like Mill, related goodness to desire, and he regarded pleasure as the primary object of desire. Hume contended that we call something "good" whenever, in contemplating it, we are pleased by it. According to his conception of the meaning of value terms, goodness is as much dependent on feeling or "sentiment" as it is on the properties of things.

The conviction of the British philosopher George Edward Moore (1873–1958), however, is different from all the preceding views. Moore insisted that goodness is a unique, unanalyzable property. According to Moore, the term "good" denotes an absolutely distinctive feature, a characteristic that cannot be understood in any other terms, either by reference to ends, desires, pleasure, or feelings of approval.

Moore's principal work on ethics is his *Principia Ethica* (1903), a work prompted by Moore's conviction that the problems of ethics have resisted resolution because of the general tendency to attempt to answer questions before making the effort to clarify the questions themselves. What Moore proposed was a careful philosophical analysis of questions concerning intrinsic goods (things that ought to exist for their own sakes) and concerning actions that ought to be performed. Prior to making the effort to consider what things might justifiably be said to be intrinsically good, Moore proposed to make clear what is meant in saying of anything whatsoever that it is good. And prior to setting forth any ideas concerning what kinds of action would be morally right, Moore proposed to clarify the ideas of duty, rightness, and obligation.

Since Moore contended that goodness is a unique and unanalyzable property, he has often been classified as an "ethical intuitionist." In the preface to *Principia Ethica*, Moore accepts that designation insofar as it pertains to his view of goodness itself. He concedes that the recognition of the goodness of something is intuitive—that is, the recognition does not depend on making deductions from evidence; one simply discovers, as a matter of direct recognition, that goodness characterizes something. But he objects to the term "intuitionist" in the description of his philosophy of right action. His contention is that actions can be *proven* to be right or wrong, even though it cannot be proven that something is intrinsically good. (He insisted, however, that one can know intuitively that there are such intrinsic goods as pleasure, knowledge, and beauty.)

Moore describes the subject-matter of ethics as consisting of whatever is common and peculiar to moral judgments involving the use of such terms as "good," "bad," "right," "wrong," and "duty." It might appear that the problems of ethics are verbal problems, in that they turn upon the definitions of certain key terms. But Moore denies that philosophy is in any way concerned with verbal questions; he suggests that problems of determining the meanings of words be left to "writers of dictionaries and other persons interested in literature . . . ." Ethics, as Moore conceives it, is "the general enquiry into what is good," and Moore explains that such an enterprise involves attempting to answer the question, "What is good?" when that question means, "What is the property denoted by the term 'good'?" and not, "What things are good?" (It may help if we regard the question as, "What is goodness?" or "What is the property denoted by the word 'good'?")

Although Moore asks, "How is good to be defined?" he denies that such a question is a verbal one. He contends that he has no interest in defining the term "good" as that term is generally used, although he states that he is inclined to think that his usage is in accord with customary usage. His problem, he reports, is that of discovering "the nature of that object or idea" that Moore himself supposes that the word "good" usually stands for.

Good as indefinable

Moore's answer to the question of the nature of goodness is admittedly "a very disappointing one." He states flatly that "good is good, and that is the end of the matter." Rephrasing the question does not help: "Or if I am asked 'How is good to be defined?' my answer is that it cannot be defined, and that is all I have to say about it."

In fact, Moore has a great deal more to say about it. He points out the importance of the claim that nothing can be said about the nature of goodness. If goodness is an unanalyzable property, if the term "good" admits of no definition, then no sentence of the form "The good is the desired"—that is, no sentence explaining what it is for something to be good—can be accepted as true. Moore denies that any such sentence can justifiably be regarded as true by definition.

Goodness cannot be analyzed, Moore argues, because it is a simple, and not a complex, property. In this respect, goodness is like yellowness (he claims), in that yellowness (unlike a horse) is simple, not complex, and thus cannot be analyzed—broken down into parts or aspects. Accordingly, the word denoting the property—namely, the word "good"—cannot be defined, for a definition is the report of an analysis of the matter denoted.

A distinction is drawn between the adjective "good," which is purportedly indefinable, and "*the* good," which would be whatever it is to which the adjective "good" applied in a case in which it could be said that "*X* is good and *X* alone is good." Moore points out that he does not deny that it may be possible to define *the* good—that is, to report the results of an analysis of that to which the adjective applies—but what he does deny is that *good* is definable (analyzable).

Analysis must eventuate in "ultimate terms," Moore argues, and consequently there is nothing peculiar in the claim that goodness is a simple and unanalyzable property. If analysis could not terminate by reference to something itself incapable of analysis, the defining process would be futile.

The naturalistic fallacy

Moore concedes that the yellow "we actually perceive"—and which is unanalyzable—can be correlated with light-vibrations that stimulate the eye, but he claims that it would be a mistake to identify the light-vibrations with yellow itself. Analogously, it is possible that the property goodness can be correlated with some other property. The view that many philosophers hold, writes Moore, that properties associated with the property goodness are to be identified with goodness, is to be named the "naturalistic fallacy."

Moore maintains that arguments which aim at the defense of definitions of "good" are either circular, trivial, or misleading. Proposed definitions are either arbitrary verbal definitions—mere stipulations of meaning—or they commit the naturalistic fallacy of presuming that the word "good" means that to which it applies as an adjective. For example, the claim that "good" means "pleasure" because the sentence "Pleasure is good " is a true sentence amounts to claiming that the sentence "Pleasure is good" means "Pleasure is pleasure"—a consequence which fails to contribute to an understanding of goodness.

Moore explains why the term "naturalistic fallacy" was chosen to designate the mistake of identifying goodness with some other property. The property denoted by the term "good," Moore claims, is not a "natural object" and, consequently, to confuse it with some other property, such as pleasure, which is a "natural object," would be to commit the fallacy of regarding as natural something (goodness) that is not natural at all. By a "natural object" Mill apparently means an object of enquiry by the natural sciences, for he contends that "Naturalism" in ethics utilizes the fallacious method of identifying goodness with "some one property or a natural object or of a collection of natural objects," and that to do so is to replace ethics "by some one of the natural sciences." (Moore argues that natural properties are distinguishable from value properties in that goodness, for example, cannot be imagined to exist "*by itself* in time," while natural properties, which are "parts of which the object is made up," seem to be able to exist independently of the existence of natural objects.)

A test of definitions

Moore offers a test for determining whether a proposed analysis of the property denoted by "good" is acceptable. He writes that "whatever definition be offered, it may be always asked, with significance, of the complex so defined, whether it is itself good." If someone were to claim, for example, that to say something is good means that it is something "we desire to desire," it would nonetheless be significant (Moore claims) to ask, "Is it good to desire to desire it?" This test disposes of any analytic proposal whatsoever, Moore insists.

If it be claimed that the term "good" is meaningless, the same test may be used to show that the claim is false. The statement "Pleasure is good" surely means more than that there is pleasure or that pleasure is pleasure, for, Moore argues, anyone asking, "Is pleasure . . . after all good?" can easily realize "that he is not merely wondering whether pleasure is pleasant."

Moore offers as an example of the naturalistic fallacy Bentham's claim that acts are right insofar as they are productive of the greatest happiness *because* the word "right" *means* "conducive to the general happiness." (Moore concedes that Bentham does not explicitly rest his case on a definition of the word "right," but he suggests that Bentham may very well have committed the naturalistic fallacy.) No reason is given for supposing that happiness is the end of action, Moore claims, if all that is claimed is that the word "right" can be defined with reference to happiness. For Bentham's view to be worth considering as an ethical proposition, it would have to establish, as a synthetic truth, the proposition that happiness is good in itself.

Having presumably established the point that the property goodness is unanalyzable and that statements about things as good in themselves must not be true by definition, Moore emphasizes the difference between questions about intrinsic goods and questions about ways of achieving what is good in itself. Statements about *means* to the good are useful as generalizations, he contends, but they are not universally true. Statements about intrinsic goods, however—that is, statements to the effect that something is good on its own account—are true whatever the circumstances and, hence, are universally true.

However, one must not make the mistake, Moore warns, of supposing that it is possible to add the values of the parts of a whole and by simple addition discover the intrinsic value of the whole. He stresses the principle that *"the value of . . . a whole bears no regular proportion to the sum of the values of its parts."*

Criticism of naturalistic ethics

In the *Principia Ethica*, Moore interrupts the exposition of his own ideas on ethics in order to undertake a critical examination of naturalistic ethics, hedonism, and metaphysical ethics. His analysis is nonetheless relevant to the discussion of goods because each of the kinds of theories considered proposes some one kind of thing as being intrinsically good, even though the theories, according to Moore, also commit the naturalistic "fallacy" of presuming that the term "good" can be defined by reference to the "natural" matter held to be good on its own account.

The terms Moore uses are not self-explanatory; in fact, they serve as technical terms to facilitate Moore's exposition. By a "naturalistic" ethics Moore means a theory of the right and the good which identifies as intrinsically good something "natural," in the sense that it is "something of which the existence is admittedly an object of experience." Within naturalistic theories, Moore distinguishes between *hedonistic* theories—those which identify pleasure as the intrinsic good—and nonhedonistic theories. By a "metaphysical" ethics Moore means an ethical theory which presumes that the good exists only "in a supersensible real world."

Moore points out that despite the fact that a metaphysical ethics goes beyond the range of experience in its search for intrinsic goods and is, in that sense, concerned with the non-natural, it is nevertheless subject to criticism as a theory which identifies goodness with the "supersensible" object and, hence, commits the "naturalistic fallacy."

Since Moore treats hedonism separately, his discussion of naturalistic ethics is limited to an appraisal of what he calls "evolutionary" ethics (after he dismisses views that identify the good with whatever is "normal" in the course of natural affairs, or "necessary," in the sense of requisite to the preservation of life). With regard to whatever is, in any of the senses mentioned, "natural," Moore contends that it always remains an open question as to whether something that happens to be the case, or necessary to life, or the product of evolutionary process is, in fact, good. The question as to whether something natural is good is certainly not to be settled by definition, he claims. And he warns against the tendency some writers have of using the term "natural" as a value term, as "when we speak of natural affections, or unnatural crimes and vices." Some method of distinguishing the good from the bad other than that of identifying events or things as "natural" is necessary in ethics, Moore concludes. (Moore is especially critical of Herbert Spencer's *Data of Ethics*, in which, according to Moore, Spencer suggests that "better" means "more evolved," and then compounds the naturalistic fallacy by apparently identifying the term "good" with the term "pleasant.")

Criticism of hedonism

Moore defines hedonism as the view that nothing is good but pleasure, and he argues that hedonists commit the naturalistic fallacy whenever they define the term "good" in terms of pleasure. Moore concedes that pleasure is an intrinsic good, but he denies that it is the sole good; and he accomplishes what he calls his "refutation" of hedonism by seeking to draw a distinction between pleasure and the *consciousness* of pleasure. Moore contends that there are many things other than pleasure (beauty, for example), such that the consciousness of them is also a good. Moore also argues that were it possible for pleasure to exist apart from the consciousness of pleasure, the pleasure "would be comparatively valueless . . . ." Consequently, he rejects the claim made by Professor Sidgwick in his *Methods of Ethics*, that beauty, knowledge, and truth are worthwhile only insofar as they are conducive, through contemplation, to happiness or the "Perfection or Excellence of human existence."

In the effort to support his contention that beauty would be worthwhile apart from any possible contemplation of it, Moore offers the following argument:

Let us imagine one world exceedingly beautiful. Imagine it as beautiful as you can; put into it whatever on this earth you most admire—mountains, rivers, the sea; trees, and sunsets, stars and moon. Imagine these all combined in the most exquisite proportions, so that no one thing jars against another, but each contributes to increase the beauty of the whole. And then imagine the ugliest world you can possibly conceive. Imagine it simply one heap of filth, containing everything that is most disgusting to us, for whatever reason, and the whole, as far as may be, without one redeeming feature . . . . The only thing we are not entitled to imagine is that any human being ever has or ever, by any possibility, *can* live in either, can ever see and enjoy the beauty of the one or hate the foulness of the other. Well, even so, supposing them quite apart from any possible contemplation by human beings; still, is it irrational to hold that it is better that the beautiful world should exist, than the one which is ugly? Would it not be well, in any case, to do what we could to produce it rather than the other? Certainly I cannot help thinking that it would . . . .

Moore argues that although a beautiful world would be of greater value were it contemplated, such a world is "in itself" better than an ugly one; beauty is, then, a part of the *summum bonum* even when it is uncontemplated.

Criticism of Mill

Mill's claim that the only proof that can be advanced to show that happiness is desirable as an end is that people actually desire it is critically challenged by Moore. Moore argues that the term "desirable" does not mean "able to be desired" but "*ought* to be desired" and that, consequently, Mill is mistaken in thinking either that desire is a sign of value or that the term "good" can be defined by reference to desire.

Moore also objects to Mill's purported distinction between the quantity and quality of pleasures. According to Moore, " 'Pleasant' must, if words are to have any meaning at all, denote some one quality common to all the things that are pleasant; and, if so, then one thing can only be more pleasant than another, according as it has more or less of this one quality." Not only is Mill mistaken, then, in supposing that it makes sense to talk about qualitative differences among pleasures, but he fails to recognize the distinction between what Moore calls "a certain excitement of some sense" (as in a case of sensual indulgence) and "the pleasure caused by such excitement." The value belongs to the "organic whole," of which pleasure, according to Moore, is only a part.

In his criticism of Sidgwick and Mill, Moore maintains that only an intuitive recognition of goods is possible. According to Moore, "Mill's judgment of preference is just a judgment of that intuitional kind which I have been contending to be necessary to establish the hedonistic or any other principle." What Moore finds objectionable, then, is not the use of intuition, but the claim that pleasures vary qualitatively and that pleasures alone determine the value of the conscious wholes of which they are parts.

Moore completes his rejection of hedonism by seeking to show that *egoistic hedonism* (the view that one's own pleasure is the sole good for the person whose pleasure it is) and *utilitarian hedonism* (the view that the greatest good is the pleasure of all concerned) are logically incompatible. (Sidgwick is criticized as attempting to allow for both positions.)

Having rejected the views that whatever is natural is good in itself, that pleasure is the sole good, and that some "supersensible reality" or a good will is the final good (as metaphysical ethics claims), Moore is prepared to examine on his own the question of determining what things are good in themselves. He contends that the method to be used in deciding whether something is good in itself is "to consider what things are such that, if they existed *by themselves*, in absolute isolation, we should yet judge their existence to be good . . . ."

Intrinsic goods

Moore quickly comes to the conclusion that pleasant states of consciousness are clearly "the most valuable things . . . ." He reaffirms his conviction that the beautiful, even when uncontemplated, has intrinsic value, but he adds that the value of a thing of beauty that is not enjoyed by anyone is as nothing compared to the value of the *consciousness* of beauty.

"Organic unities" consisting of complex states of conscious enjoyments provide moral philosophy with its *raison d'être*, according to Moore. He insists that "it is only for the sake of these things—in order that as much of them as possible may at some time exist—that anyone can be justified in performing any public or private duty; . . . these complex wholes *themselves*, and not any constituent or characteristic of them . . . form the rational ultimate end of human action and the sole criterion of social progress . . . ." He adds that "personal affections and aesthetic enjoyments include *all* the greatest, and *by far* the greatest, goods we can imagine . . . ."

Moore resists the hedonistic injunction to abstract from complex states of enjoyment the pleasure which presumably pervades such states and endows them with intrinsic value. He contends that "the whole 'enjoyment' owes its value quite equally to the presence of the other constituents, *even though* it may be true that the pleasure is the only constituent having any value by itself."

In the appreciation of beauty there is not only an emotional element, but also a cognitive one, Moore suggests. And although the enjoyment of beauty would be of little value without the emotional element, the feeling itself would lose most or all of its value were it not part of the organic whole consisting of the cognitive and emotional responses to the thing of beauty.

Moore considers the question whether the actual existence of an object believed to exist and enjoyed as existing adds to the value of the enjoyment of that object. His conclusion is that even when one does not add to the value of the enjoyment the value of the independently existing object itself, the enjoyment of an actually existent object is more valuable, as an organic whole, than would be the enjoyment occasioned by a "purely imaginative appreciation." Consequently, Moore believes those philosophers to be justified who have maintained that *knowledge* has intrinsic value.

A definition of "beautiful" is proposed by which, Moore claims, the naturalistic fallacy of identifying the beautiful with whatever "produces certain effects upon our feelings" is avoided: "It appears probable that the beautiful should be *defined* as that of which the admiring contemplation is good in itself." Moore adds that "to say that a thing is beautiful is to say, not indeed that it is *itself* good, but that it is a necessary element in something which is: to prove that a thing is truly beautiful is to prove that a whole, to which it bears a particular relation as a part, is truly good."

In addition to aesthetic enjoyments, which comprise one of the two classes of "great unmixed goods," there are "the pleasures of human intercourse or of personal affection . . . ." The enjoyment of persons involves not only the elements necessary to aesthetic enjoyment—namely, emotion, cognition, and knowledge—but also the intrinsic value of the person who constitutes the object of affection. Both the mental and bodily qualities of the person loved contribute to the value of the enjoyment of that person, although, Moore contends, the mental qualities can be grasped, it seems, only through the recognition of certain bodily expressions.

Philosophical idealists have been mistaken, Moore suggests, in regarding the *summum bonum* as being exclusively spiritual. A whole experience involving the appreciation of "material qualities" is superior in value to one which consists in the appreciation (if possible) of spiritual goods alone.

Just as intrinsic goods are organic unities involving cognitive and emotional elements, intrinsic evils are organic wholes in which both cognition and emotion play a part. There are three kinds of "positive evils," according to Moore's classification: the enjoyment of what is evil or ugly, the hatred of what is good or beautiful, and pains. Since by "pain" Moore means "the consciousness of pain," it follows, as he points out, that pain *by itself* is an evil and is thus an exception to the general rule that intrinsic goods and evils are organic unities involving both cognition and an emotional attitude toward an object.

Throughout his discussion of intrinsic goods, Moore emphasizes both the crucial role of consciousness and the distinctive feature of organic unities (that the value of a whole is usually not to be identified with the sum of the values of the parts). Thus, beauty is intrinsically good, but the consciousness of beauty is immeasurably better; the enjoyment of beauty and of persons may contain elements of pleasure, but the value of the entire experience is much greater than the sum of the parts. Moore maintains that even evil can contribute to the value of a whole, as is the case whenever the evil of retributive punishment results in a state of affairs less bad than would have been the case had the crime (which is itself evil) gone unpunished. And certain mixed goods, such as instances of courage and compassion, can exist as valuable wholes only as responses to evil.

Morally obligatory acts

Moore also deals with the question of determining what kind of conduct is morally right or obligatory. He contends, "the assertion 'I am morally bound to perform this action' is identical with the assertion 'This action will produce the greatest possible amount of good in the Universe' . . . . " If an act *ought* to be done, Moore argues, then "the whole world will be better, if it be performed, than if any possible alternative were taken." An act is morally right if it "will *not* cause *less* good than any possible alternative."

Moore categorically rejects the claim that moral laws or rules are discoverable through intuition. Intuition reveals whatever is good in itself, but it cannot reveal the kinds of action that yield the greatest benefit.

Nor is it possible through causal investigation, however thorough, to decide with complete assurance what our duty is, Moore maintains. Consequently, in appraising alternative courses of action, a person cannot reasonably be expected to do more than give careful attention to the *most likely* courses of action and consider which among them would, if undertaken, produce the most good. Moore concedes that absolute certainty, even with regard to the immediate consequences of an action, is not possible, and that generalizations concerning the usual benefits of acts are therefore particularly helpful.

Since whatever is our duty is, according to Moore, a means to good, the common distinction between duty and expediency cannot be maintained. However, he concedes, one tends to use the word "duty"· only in those cases of utility in which there is a "moral sentiment" of approval or disapproval, and with reference to acts which, as affecting others more than ourselves, we may be "strongly tempted to omit." In other words, if an act is clearly for our benefit, we are naturally inclined to perform it, and although we may describe it as "expedient," we do not tend to designate it as a "duty." If, on the other hand, we recognize the utility of an act as having obvious beneficial effects on others and yet are tempted, because of personal considerations, to avoid the act, we tend to call it a "duty."

Virtues must also be related to acts productive of the good if virtue is to be of any worth, Moore claims. Virtue has no value in itself but derives whatever value it has from its tendency, as a habitual disposition to do what is right, to be productive of the good.

In many respects Moore's ethics resembles that of Mill, in that there is the same emphasis upon the utility of acts and the same tendency to regard agreeable conscious states as good in themselves. However, Moore resists any final commitment to hedonism and argues that pleasure is only one element in those "organic unities" consisting of the enjoyment of complex situations. Furthermore, Moore rejects any analysis of value which terminates in a reference to desire or to any "natural" thing. Although, in agreement with the Utilitarian, he not only denies that one can discover any formal principles of conduct through intuition, but also relates the value of actions exclusively to the production of good, at the same time he regards the discovery of intrinsic goods to be possible only through intuition. His main point is that goodness is an unanalyzable and hence indefinable property and that, consequently, any attempt to explain goodness by relating it to something other than goodness represents what he calls "the naturalistic fallacy."

AYER: VALUE TERMS
AS EMOTIVE TERMS

Professor Alfred Jules Ayer, in *Language, Truth and Logic* (1936), defends an account of value terms which is reminiscent of Hume's view that moral judgment is determined by sentiment. But Ayer's position is clearly different in that he maintains that so-called moral judgments and value claims are *not* meaningful expressions of propositions that are either true or false. Statements containing value terms are emotively expressive, he insists. Such statements reveal the attitude of the speaker, but they say nothing about the objects to which they refer, except to indicate that the objects are objects toward which certain feelings are directed.

Ayer's analysis of value statements is within the context of a many-faceted critical examination of the contention that some synthetic propositions (propositions such that the predicate term is not part of the meaning of the subject term) are nonempirical. The author purports to show that all synthetic judgments are indeed empirical—based upon experience or relating to matters open to experience. He alludes to the claim that perhaps value judgments comprise a class of exceptions, for it appears to many critics of the extreme empiricism (logical positivism) that Ayer contends that "statements of value" are synthetic propositions which cannot be understood as hypotheses predicting the course of sense experience.

The emotive function of normative symbols

Ayer agrees that some statements about values are significant (empirically meaningful), but he claims that insofar as such statements are significant, they are so in a "scientific" way—that is, as indicating the consequences of action. But when one turns to "normative ethical symbols"—to such terms as "good" and "bad," "right" and "wrong"—one finds that such terms, as used in moral judgments, cannot be "translated" into empirical terms. Both the subjectivist (who claims that moral judgments tell us what actions are generally approved of) and the utilitarian (who understands by the rightness of an act its tendency to promote happiness) are mistaken, Ayer argues, for it is not self-contradictory to say, with regard to acts approved of or tending toward happiness, that they are bad or wrong. Thus, the effort to *define* value terms or ethical terms by interpreting such terms as giving information about the consequences of acts or the attitudes or feelings of persons must fail.

Ayer distinguishes between what he calls "normative" symbols and "descriptive" symbols, and he cautions the reader that his account of the emotive function of moral terms is confined to the normative symbols. If one uses the term "wrong" to report what kind of action is frowned upon in a certain group or society, the term is used descriptively; but if one uses the term to pass judgment on a mode of action, the term is used normatively.

Ayer also makes it clear that his account is limited to "the conventions of our actual language." He acknowledges that a language might be devised which would permit a translation of ethical terms into nonethical terms, but he insists that the actual normative use of value terms in moral judgments cannot be understood through relating the terms to sense experience. Hence he states incisively, "Our contention is simply that *in our language*, sentences which contain normative ethical symbols are not equivalent to sentences which express psychological propositions, or indeed empirical propositions of any kind." (Italics added.)

Ethical intuitionists contend that it is possible, by a kind of direct, nonrational insight, to discover the value of certain ways of conduct, and such persons argue that although moral judgments are consequently not verifiable in terms of sense experience, they are nevertheless synthetic, meaningful judgments. But Ayer insists throughout his book that synthetic judgments are meaningful only to the degree that they can be understood by reference to the sense experiences that would verify them. Accordingly he argues that unless moral judgments are analyzable empirically, they are not significant.

Ethical concepts as "pseudo-concepts"

Although Ayer agrees with the "absolutist" or intuitionist in ethics in thinking that moral judgments are not analyzable, he attributes the unanalyzability of such judgments not to a unique, intuitable subject-matter, but to the fact that such judgments involve ethical concepts that are "mere pseudo-concepts." When someone claims that an act is "wrong," he does not give any information about the act; he merely evinces a disapproval of it. A "moral judgment" does not even *state* that the act judged is one that provokes or meets with moral approval or disapproval; it simply reveals the feelings of the speaker.

A critical consequence of Ayer's view, as he points out, is that moral judgments, although resembling factual propositions, have no truth value—they are neither true or false. Ethical disagreements are not disagreements about matters of fact; they merely reveal differences in moral sentiments.

Confusion arises concerning the function of ethical symbols because they are often used in conjunction with factual claims. A sentence which is in part a description of a certain empirical matter may contain a value term that expresses the speaker's feeling with regard to the matter described, and one is easily led to suppose that the value term is itself factual and descriptive. But, writes Ayer, "in every case in which one would commonly be said to be making an ethical judgment, the function of the relevant ethical word is purely 'emotive.' "

The emotive function of ethical symbols is not exclusively expressive, Ayer argues. Such symbols may be used to arouse feeling and thereby to incite action. Sentences containing ethical terms so used may have the appearance of factual claims, but they function as injunctions; they serve as commands. Various expressions may be ranged according to the forcefulness of the command implicit in their use:

Thus the sentence "It is your duty to tell the truth" may be regarded both as the expression of a certain sort of ethical feeling about truthfulness and as the expression of the command "Tell the truth." The sentence "You ought to tell the truth" also involves the command "Tell the truth," but here the tone of the command is less emphatic. In the sentence "It is good to tell the truth" the command has become little more than a suggestion.

One may accordingly distinguish the "meanings" of various ethical symbols by differentiating their expressive and injunctive functions.

Factual discourse and ethical discourse

Ayer does not deny that discourse about feelings and attitudes is possible; in fact, as he points out, such discourse is common. But a distinction must be made, he contends, between *factual* discourse *about* feelings and *ethical* discourse *expressive* of feelings. The emotive theory of value is superior to that of the subjectivist, Ayer argues, because the emotive theory allows for differences of attitude, while the subjectivist theory attempts to relate the validity of ethical judgments to feelings. The emotivist theory succeeds precisely because it does not attempt to establish such a relation; the theory denies altogether the validity of ethical judgments.

Ayer refers to Moore's critical comment that if ethical judgments are simply statements about feelings (as the subjectivists claim), argument about values is impossible (for each party to a dispute can acknowledge the difference in feeling and yet be insistent in his judgment). Ayer's reply to Moore's objection (which is seen as applying also to Ayer's emotivist theory) is that disputes about values are indeed possible, but such disputes are not about feelings; they are about matters of fact related to feelings.

Ayer points out that disputes about moral matters are usually the result of differences of opinion with regard to motives, actual happenings, or the circumstances surrounding actions. Once such differences of opinion are settled, agreement is possible whenever the parties to the dispute have received a similar "moral education"— that is, whenever they tend to feel much the same way about conduct. But if the basic feelings with regard to conduct differ, argument is futile and is consequently abandoned.

The province of ethics

What is the proper province of ethics, then, if ethical judgments are nothing more than emotive utterances involving the use of "pseudo-concepts"? Ayer argues that ethics—"ethical philosophy"—should be limited to the attempt to define ethical terms. The study of moral experience belongs either to psychology or sociology. Exhortations to virtue are not propositional in character and cannot, then, constitute the body of any philosophy or science. Since an examination of the uses of ethical terms shows that such terms are used emotively, either to express feelings or to incite action through arousing feeling, the entire content of ethics, according to Ayer, consists of the claim that ethical concepts, in that their function is emotive, are unanalyzable pseudo-concepts.

Ayer's position with regard to the function of ethical terms leads him to reject, then, problems of ethics which, for other philosophers are central: the problem of discovering what, in fact, is good on its own account; and the problem of discovering what, in fact, is the fundamental moral law. There are no such factual matters, Ayer claims, and hence there are no such problems of ethics.

Ayer suggests that the "categorical" force of moral imperatives derives from the fear evoked by the belief that failure to act in certain ordained ways will provoke the anger of some god or the enmity of society. Other moral generalizations are convincing because they incorporate conclusions concerning the most effective means for securing one's own happiness or the satisfaction of society's needs or objectives. But, concludes Ayer, any philosopher who attempts to clarify the meanings of ethical terms by relating them to a metaphysical ground of moral obligation or to the tendency of certain actions to be productive of happiness confuses the problem of determining the causes of moral feelings with the problem of defining ethical terms.

The emphasis upon an examination of the functions of ethical terms, central to Ayer's philosophical performance in ethics, is characteristic of a dominant tendency in contemporary philosophy. The problems of ethics have become for many philosophers the problems of ethical language.

DISCUSSION
QUESTIONS

1. Is a teacher of ethics a teacher of morality?
2. If the claim is made that values and duties are known intuitively, is there any way of disputing that claim?
3. How is it possible for a man to do something above and beyond the call of duty?
4. Can a man be wrong who conscientiously acts "on principle"?
5. Does the fact that an act is customary tend to make that act morally right?
6. Is the term "moral," as used in such expressions as "morally right" and "morally obligatory," a value term?
7. Can a value term be both subjectively expressive and objectively descriptive?
8. Is it possible for a man to be in a situation in which he has no moral obligation whatsoever?
9. Would a man living in isolation have any moral obligations?
10. Are there any universal values or universal duties?
11. Is what Moore calls a "naturalistic fallacy" a fallacy?
12. If the categorical "ought" is a conditional "would" (see Kant), isn't the moral "ought" somewhat conditional?
13. If, relative to someone who is dead, death is a good, is that value instrumental or intrinsic?
14. Is knowledge necessary to virtue? Is knowledge sufficient to virtue?

ADDITIONAL
READINGS

Bentham, Jeremy. *Principles of Morals and Legislation*, 1789.
Broad, Charlie Dunbar. *Five Types of Ethical Theory*, 1930.
Butler, Joseph. *Fifteen Sermons Preached at the Rolls Chapel*, 1726.
Dewey, John. *Human Nature and Conduct*, 1922.
——. *The Theory of Valuation*, 1939.
Green, Thomas Hill. *Prolegomena to Ethics*, 1883.
Lewis, Clarence Irving. *An Analysis of Knowledge and Valuation*, 1946.
——. *The Ground and Nature of the Right*, 1955.
McGreal, Ian. *The Art of Making Choices*, 1953.
Nietzsche, Friedrich Wilhelm. *Beyond Good and Evil*, 1886.
——. *Thus Spake Zarathustra*, 1885.
Perry, Ralph Barton. *General Theory of Value*, 1926.
Ross, Sir David. *The Right and the Good*, 1930.
——. *Foundations of Ethics*, 1939.
Schlick, Moritz. *Problems of Ethics*, 1930.
Sellars, Wilfred, and John Hospers. *Readings in Ethical Theory*, 1952.
Sharp, Frank Chapman. *Ethics*, 1928.
Sidgwick, Henry. *The Methods of Ethics*, 1901.
Spinoza, Benedictus de. *Ethics*, 1677.
Stevenson, Charles L. *Ethics and Language*, 1944.
Lepley, Ray (ed.). *Value: A Cooperative Inquiry*, 1949.
——. *The Language of Value*, 1957.
Prichard, H. A. *Moral Obligation*, 1949.

INDEX

113